Are You
Following Jesus
or Just
Fooling Around?!

Dr. Ray Cummings

ACKNOWLEDGEMENTS

- The first and foremost thanks and praise goes to My Lord and Savior, Jesus Christ. Without You, Lord, I would be nothing!
- Thanks Amanda for being my beloved Wife. You are my inspiration and my invigoration. Thank you for allowing me to be involved in your life. (Thanks, also, for keeping me straight spiritually when I start fooling around!)
- Thanks to the greatest thing that ever happened to me after salvation and marriage: my son, Carter Reed Cummings, and second son, Camron Brady Cummings, to come in April of 2003! You are such a blessing from God! You bring unending joy to both Amanda and myself!
- Thanks to my family that raised me.
  - To My Dad – Richard Cummings – for all your advice, fatherly love, and godly example.

- To My Mom – Vivian Cummings – for all your encouragement, patience, and motherly love.
- To My Twin Brother – Dr. Ricky Cummings – for being my best friend all our lives, for spiritually pushing me, and for serving alongside me at Providence Baptist Church!
- To My Sister – Stephanie Brown – for keeping me straight growing up, for your constant support, and love.
- Thanks to Providence Baptist Church – What a great Family of Faith! In a world full of churches and Christians fooling around, so many of you are truly seeking to follow Jesus. Thanks for allowing me to serve my first pastorate with you (mistakes and all), and for encouraging me in the writing of my first book!
- Thanks to Jonathan H. Lucenay – a childhood friend. Thanks for your personal and prayerful support of this book and your love for God's Kingdom!
- And last but not least – thanks to Garren and Annabeth Bates. Your friendship means the world to Amanda and myself. And thanks Annabeth for all your proofreading and helpful corrections.

FOREWORD

Ray Cummings writes from the overflow of his heart and conveys an authentic desire to exalt Jesus Christ. He focuses his passion upon the naked truth that believers today stand at a fork in the road. They can choose the appealing path of compromise or they can take the arduous path of conviction. As Ray would say, "You can fool around or you can follow Jesus!"

He is on target about our responsibility to get off the sidelines and get into the game. I shutter when I consider how the church today is spiritually out of shape. Too many of us prefer sampling God's Word and too few of us enjoy digesting His truth. We shun the discipline of daily faithfulness and seek the delight of occasional ecstasies. Ray reminds us that nothing less than humble obedience lies at the heart of following Jesus. Anything less places us in the category of "fooling around."

Dr. Dean Register
Pastor - Temple Baptist Church - Hattiesburg, MS.

In these pages, Ray Cummings has opened "the" book, has opened his heart, and has opened the doors to some of our churches. Additionally, he has opened a mental window through which breezes of fresh thought can flow.

Recently, I was visiting with one of our pastors in the state who was serving at his first church. He was relating to me that he was not particularly thrilled over the fact that one of the older ladies in this church had told him that he was "green." Here he was – called, obviously gifted by God, college educated and seminary trained, and leading his first church, and a member would assess that he was "green!" As he talked with me, I was thinking, but not saying, "Man, what a great thing!" You see, I was recalling a description that was given about an old pastor in the early years of my ministry and they said of him, "All of his life he has stayed 'green' between the ears." I understood that then and after almost 40 years have passed, I understand it even more now.

It is so easy to slip into life's ruts where exciting daily activities become routine, then the routine becomes repeated sameness, and the sameness begins to turn a brown color signifying that life has gone and there only remains a structure. When that takes place, a person is living close to the cemetery. Now, he or she may not die, but you can watch for the death of thought, death of creativity, death of excitement, and the growth has stopped.

In this book, Ray Cummings has brought to us interesting and new streams of thought. Using a play on words, he does not play with the work of the Lord, using practical, sometimes very thought provoking terms. He walks with us through some of our churches and many of our hearts. He touches one nerve after another and often reminds us of the spiritual schizophrenia that at times marks our lives.

You will be blessed as you read, for at times you will run into folks you know, situations you have experienced, and you may even smile. But, then your smile may fade as you get a glimpse of the mirror just out of the corner of your eye and see yourself.

May God bless this book to enable more of us to grow in our walk and be more serious about following Jesus.

Prayerfully yours,
Jim Futral
Executive Director
Treasurer of the Mississippi Baptist Convention Board

CONTENTS

Introduction

"Oxymorons for Spiritual Morons"

Bum Phillips, the once football coach for the Houston Oilers, was asked by a reporter if Earl Campbell was the greatest running back to ever play professional football. Bum Phillips responded, *"He might not be in a class by himself, but it doesn't take long to call the roll."* [1] To find Christians today that are committed to Jesus and are truly following Him is extremely hard. The class is small and it doesn't take long to call the roll! *"Are We Following Jesus or Just Fooling Around?"*

A young boy who had misbehaved was ordered by his mother to stand in the corner for a few moments of "time out" and contemplate the nature of his behavior. After arguing for a few minutes the young boy relented and said, *"OK, I will go; my body will be there but my heart won't!"* [2] How true. How true. For some of us, our bodies are in the church on Sundays, yet our heart is nowhere in sight. Christians all across the world need to ask themselves the question, *"Are we* truly *following Jesus, or* are we truly *just fooling around?!"*

> *Washington's Playhouse once sponsored a two-week run of "The Mark of the Hawk." The 80-minute color film represented an effort by a preeminent Presbyterian Church in the US to create public interest in missions. Actress Eartha Kitt played a lead role.*
>
> *Three months later, Miss Kitt was back on the Playhouse screen in a different film. This time she played the role of a prostitute in United Artist's "Anna Lucasta."* [3]

Many Christians today are playing dual roles in their relationship with Christ: following Jesus on Sundays and fooling around the rest of the week! Like the nation of Israel, we are God's chosen people, and yet, we have committed spiritual adultery as the bride of Christ. *"Are we really following Jesus or just fooling around?"*

Hopefully, throughout this book, the Lord will shed some light on the inconsistencies of our spiritual lives. I have chosen some oxymorons through which God revealed to me that, in many ways, I am a spiritual moron. Maybe the Lord will convict you in the same way. Webster defines an oxymoron as *"a figure of speech in which opposite or contradictory ideas or terms are combined."* Webster also defines an oxymoron as *"a smart saying which at first appears foolish."* The word comes from two words: *oxys* which means "sharp" and *moros* which means "dull" or "foolish."[4] In other words, God has led me to title each chapter with some, hopefully, sharp evaluations that may lead many of us to feel foolish about our spiritual progress in this life. At the end of each chapter, I have contrasted the actions of many Christians with the character of Christ as seen in God's Word. The goal of this work is that when we see our inconsistencies in light of God's unchanging character, we would be ready to follow God's Word in Ephesians 5:1-2:

> *1 Be imitators of God, therefore, as dearly loved children 2 and live a life of love, just as Christ loved us and gave himself up for us as a fragrant offering and sacrifice to God.*

May God allow you to be honest with yourself as you personalize this book by seeking to answer the question: *"Am I Following Jesus or Just Fooling Around?"*

CHAPTER 1

"Consistently Inconsistent"

CHAPTER TRUTH:

Christians consistently find excuses for not worshipping God, but then they do not hold to those same excuses when it comes to other loves of their lives.

I often find it amazing how inconsistent people can be in their lives. What I mean is that people make all kinds of excuses for not coming to worship yet will put up with almost anything in other areas of their lives. The following examples are but a few instances that prove this truth. I saw several of these just this week.

- A man has not been in Sunday School for a month, because he did not like a comment made to him in Sunday School. Yet he came to the first church softball practice with a hurt shoulder. In other words, he loved softball enough to practice with a hurt shoulder, but did not love Jesus enough to get over his hurt feelings!

- Another man has not been in church for months, because he did not like a decision the deacons made. Yet he yelled at the umpire's decision to call his grandson out on strikes. He did not get up and leave the ballgame when he disagreed with the umpire's decision. In other words, he could put up with a bad call to watch his grandson, but he couldn't get over a disagreement to worship God's Son! (I hope and pray that the Divine Umpire doesn't call him out one day!!)

- A lady complains that we stand too long when we sing praises to God, yet she stands three times as long in the checkout line at Wal-Mart. In other words, she is hungry enough for food to stand, but when it comes to the bread of life, she will sit! Maybe that would change if she realized that Jesus checked out her stand (or lack of it) for Him!

- People complain that they cannot come to worship on Sunday night because it is too late for their kids (we get out at 8:00 PM), but those same parents and kids are playing Dixie Youth Baseball until 10:00 PM on Tuesday nights. I guess that time is not the real factor. Rather, certain things are worth staying up late for, and worshipping the Savior of our lives is not one of them!

- Some people believe that it is wrong to get emotionally excited in worship, yet those same people go nuts cheering for their favorite team on Friday nights. Maybe they think it is more exciting if their team comes out of a slump than they do about Jesus coming out of the tomb! Or maybe they think it is more exciting that their star player ran over a safety and a defensive back than the fact that Jesus ran over sin, death, hell, and the grave! (Just a thought!!) Oh by the way, they shout and scream for a team that may lose, while they soak and sour about the Christ who has already won!

- Some people are highly concerned that we don't have enough grave plots for people when they die. Yet they don't show the same concern that we don't have enough parking places to enable people to come in and get to know Jesus – The Giver of Life! Does a saved man need a grave plot more than a lost man needs the Living Lord? Does a dead man need a 6-foot by 4-foot stretch of dirt more than a lost man needs a Savior and Deliverer? Doesn't a twice born man die only once while a once born man dies twice? It seems to me that we wouldn't need as many graves if we had more twice born people! (Exaggerated a tad bit, but it helps you see my point.)

- At times, I see emergencies bring forth inconsistencies in our walk of faith. People who never depend on the church for anything suddenly contact the church for prayer and ministry when a crisis hits their family. When times are good, these people see no need for God or His church.

In other words, they see no need for their family of faith. However, when a tragedy strikes, their family of faith becomes the most important thing in their life. As the urgency of the situation increases, so does their dependency on God and His church. Don't these people realize that the greatest tragedy of all is not death? Rather, the greatest tragedy is for one to die without Christ! And another tragedy is to live and never really have lived life abundantly.

- A woman has not been in church for a year, because she states her bad health as an excuse. Yet, an old friend had a heart attack, and this woman spent hours a day for a solid week at the hospital comforting the family. Often, she stands against the wall in the ICU waiting room for over an hour. Her health seems to be cured when it comes to ministering to the family of a loved one. But this same lady cannot muster enough faith to honor the Beloved One. Doesn't she realize that there has never been a loved one who can love her like the Lord of Love?!

- And then, there are the couples that insist on getting married in a church, yet they never attend church before or after the wedding. Could it be that they want to make their commitment in a church and not to The Christ?! Or could it be that they want their wedding day to be great but they could care less if their marriage was godly?! Maybe their marriage is on "holey" ground because their wedding day was the only thing on "holy" ground?

- That reminds me of the parents who never attend church, but they want their children dedicated to the Lord via a Baby Dedication. The church seems to be a spectacular place to dedicate their baby, but the same church is not significant enough to raise their baby under the teaching of the Lord. Could it be that they would rather have a Bible engraved with their baby's name on it rather than have the Bible engraved on the Baby's heart?! Or could it be that a certificate of dedication means more to them that the certainty of salvation?! Or possibly, the parents would rather have a one-time family dedication rather than an all-time family determination to seek the Lord!

Now, I do want you readers to understand that this long list of excuses is not listed here out of frustration of church membership or attendance. It would not frustrate this pastor at all if these people got upset with me or the church and went and worshipped faithfully somewhere else. What bothers me is that these people do not worship God anywhere on any given Sunday! God did not save me and call me to grow a great church, but to serve a Great Christ. Christ did not ordain me as a pastor to have the largest church in the convention, but to share the gospel in order to grow the Kingdom! I am not a Company Man, I am a Kingdom Man. And I cannot understand what these excuses have to do with a God who would send His Only Son to give them eternal life! Therefore, these excuse are just that – excuses that lead people away from Christ and His sacrifice for them on the cross at Calvary.

Christians definitely have a tendency to be consistently inconsistent. We say that we cannot attend church for all these various reasons, but we go to the mall, play ball, and, basically, do all the things that we wish to do. I believe that we do what we desire to do. If we love it enough, we will play ball at all times of the night. Take for example, a group of men who will play a softball tournament all night long in order to bring home the first place trophy. Yet if Jesus was first place in our lives, we would stay up all night, if need be, to get a word from Him. It boils down to one's passion. A person will go the greatest extremes for what they are the most passionate about. Possibly, that is the reason that Jesus listed the greatest commandment in Matthew 22:37-38:

> *37 Jesus replied: "Love the Lord your God with all your heart and with all your soul and with all your mind." 38 This is the first and greatest commandment.*

Jesus knew that the heart of the matter was a matter of the heart!

I am so glad that Jesus is Consistently Consistent! God's Word says in Hebrews 13:8 that:

8 Jesus Christ is the same yesterday and today and forever.

God never changes. He is the only constant in our lives that are surrounded with inconsistencies!

Another passage that needs to be mentioned concerning God's unchanging nature is Matthew 6:26-30:

26 Look at the birds of the air; they do not sow or reap or store away in barns, and yet your heavenly Father feeds them. Are you not much more valuable than they? 27 Who of you by worrying can add a single hour to his life? 28 "And why do you worry about clothes? See how the lilies of the field grow. They do not labor or spin. 29 Yet I tell you that not even Solomon in all his splendor was dressed like one of these. 30 If that is how God clothes the grass of the field, which is here today and tomorrow is thrown into the fire, will he not much more clothe you, O you of little faith?

God cares for the birds of the air and the flowers of the field enough to feed the birds and clothe the grass with beautiful flowers. But God's Passion is People, and He so loved the world that He sent His Son to die for people, not birds or flowers. We are the heart-of-the-matter for Jesus, and we are the matter of His heart. If we, then, are most important in this world to Jesus, shouldn't He be most important to us?! And shouldn't our actions reveal to a lost world that we love Jesus more than anything else?! I believe the greatest commandment is Jesus' answer to that question!

I have a son who is 2 years old. I now understand how my own father felt about me. The one thing I want most for my son, Carter, is the one thing that my father wanted most for me. He wanted me to confess my faith in Jesus Christ and then to be consistent in that walk of faith. I do not know of one parent that wants his son or daughter to be inconsistent. No parent in his or her right mind would want a son or daughter who used drugs and alcohol throughout the week, yet still went to church on Sunday. Going to church on Sunday would, in no way, cancel out the child's lifestyle in the mind of his parents. Likewise, going to church on Sunday, in no way, cancels out our lifestyle in the mind of our Heavenly Father.

Since Jesus is Consistently Consistent, He desires the same for His children. So, as Christians, we need to start living throughout the week what we say "Amen" to on Sunday. Our worship needs to match up with our walk, or else we just need to quit trying to fool everybody, because God is not fooled one bit with our inconsistencies.

CHAPTER 2

"Graciously Unforgiving"

CHAPTER TRUTH:

Many Christians have made an art form out of receiving grace from God while not showing any of that grace to others!

Christians often are the first ones to appreciate God's grace yet the last ones to forgive others. Jesus spilled out His blood to forgive our sins, and we respond by splitting up His church with unforgiveness. Have we forgotten the words of Jesus in Matthew 6:14-15?

> *14 For if you forgive men when they sin against you, your heavenly Father will also forgive you. 15 But if you do not forgive men their sins, your Father will not forgive your sins.*

Don't we realize that our forgiveness towards others is directly related to God's forgiveness of our sins? How could we receive God's grace and not extend forgiveness?

Just imagine God's audible response to our judgmental

thoughts next time you are tempted to be unforgiving.

"I can't believe she would show her face in church."
God – "Don't you know that I died so that she could find grace in Christ?"

"He acts like we don't know the sin in his life."
God – "You act like I don't know the sin in your life!"

"He was out last night drunk with a woman that wasn't his wife."
God – "Thank goodness, He listened to My voice and came to church tonight."

"She thinks that she is so holy, because she does all that for the church."
God – "I wish you would strive to be holy and submit and serve Your Christ."

"I will never forgive him for what he did to me."
God – "What if I felt the same way about your sin? If so, there would be no Calvary!"

Forgiven and Never Forgiving is like:
Being loved and never loving.
Being found and never looking.
Given sight and never seeing.
Having hands and never reaching.
Being born and never really living!

It leads me to wonder:
How could we be so blinded to our Savior's grace?
How could we throw His Love for us back in His face?
How could we be forgiven, yet no grace abound?
Because we are not following Jesus, we're just fooling
around!!

In Scripture, Jesus always took present day situations to reveal our times of fooling around. Let's do the same with the area of unforgiving Christians.

Imagine you have made some major financial mistakes. Because of your high-risk living, you have plunged so deeply into the water of woes that you are desperately drowning. In fact, your family has no idea you gambled and lost the family's savings. Then, to pay it back, your borrowed from a loan shark. You thought you would try your luck again with the borrowed money, yet you lost it all on a boat not too far from shore. The shark came to shallow waters to collect what he was owed. In the meantime, you had become pretty shallow yourself, and yet, you were way over your head. To sum it all up, you now owed in excess of $20 Million Dollars!! You didn't need a lifeguard; you needed to win the lottery!

So when the loan shark found you bleeding, you did what anybody would do. In the middle of fear, frustration, and failure, you begged for your life. And then when it couldn't get any worse, suddenly it couldn't get any better. Because the loan shark that had come to collect, saw that you couldn't splash out of your situation if you lived an extra 1,000 years. So the loan shark did the unthinkable. He said these words to you, "You don't have to pay back a dime." You can't believe your ears. A shark would find you in bloody water and not even nibble at your toe! You owed $20 million dollars, and you don't have to pay back one "red" "bloody" cent! Unbelievable!

So, what do you do now that you aren't drowning? What do you do when the weight of the world has been lifted off of your shoulders and you are finally standing on solid ground? You remember that twenty years ago, Bob lost a bet with you for $20! No way. You, who were just forgiven a debt of over $20 million dollars, are now upset because Bob never paid you back the $20 he owed you?! Unbelievable?! Even more unbelievable than being forgiven a dept that you could never pay!!

"An unlikely story", you say. "Why would you even hypothetically give such a never-going-to-happen situation," you smirk. Because it was precisely God's response to Peter in Matthew 18:

> *21 Then Peter came to Jesus and asked, "Lord, how many times shall I forgive my brother when he sins against me? Up to seven times?" 22 Jesus answered, "I tell you, not seven times, but seventy-seven times. 23 "Therefore, the kingdom of heaven is like a king who wanted to settle accounts with his servants. 24 As he*

began the settlement, a man who owed him ten thousand talents was brought to him. 25 Since he was not able to pay, the master ordered that he and his wife and his children and all that he had be sold to repay the debt. 26 "The servant fell on his knees before him. 'Be patient with me,' he begged, 'and I will pay back everything.' 27 The servant's master took pity on him, canceled the debt and let him go. 28 "But when that servant went out, he found one of his fellow servants who owed him a hundred denarii. He grabbed him and began to choke him. 'Pay back what you owe me!' he demanded. 29 "His fellow servant fell to his knees and begged him, 'Be patient with me, and I will pay you back.' 30 "But he refused. Instead, he went off and had the man thrown into prison until he could pay the debt. 31 When the other servants saw what had happened, they were greatly distressed and went and told their master every-thing that had happened. 32 "Then the master called the servant in. 'You wicked servant,' he said, 'I canceled all that debt of yours because you begged me to. 33 Shouldn't you have

> *had mercy on your fellow servant just as I had on you?' 34 In anger his master turned him over to the jailers to be tortured, until he should pay back all he owed. 35 "This is how my heavenly Father will treat each of you unless you forgive your brother from your heart."*

You see the only difference between my scenario and Jesus' story is that in my scenario, there was a loan shark. In Jesus' story, there was a lone Savior! But in both cases, there existed a man who owed a debt he could not pay. And we all owe Jesus for the grace that covered the wages of our sin. We owed death; Jesus paid it and gave us life!

Did you hear verses 34-35? I mean, when you read it, were you really listening, or were you just reading? If the first time you read it, you were fooling around, really listen to it this time.

> *34 In anger his master turned him over to the jailers to be tortured, until he should pay back all he owed. 35 "This is how my heavenly Father will treat each of you unless you forgive your brother from your heart."*

Listening?! Do we really want to be unforgiving? Do we really want the Father to treat us the same way

38

we treat so many people?! Do we really want to be turned back over to the jailer of this world and be entrapped by sin again until we can pay back all that we owe?! In other words, do we want to live forever entrapped by the sin of bitterness, because we can't express forgiveness to others after receiving God's grace to us?!

The most selfish thing a Christian can do is ask for God's grace without being willing for others to find God's grace too! How many people are we leaving lost because we can't learn to forgive? I really believe that if lost people didn't have to stumble over unforgiving Christians, they would have a much easier path to the grace of God!

Aren't you so glad that God is not like us! Most of the time, we are gracefully unforgiving. Yet, Jesus is graciously forgiving! His Word says that where sin abounded, grace abounded even more. Romans 5:20-21 reads:

> *20 The law was added so that the trespass might increase. But where sin increased, grace increased all the more, 21 so that, just as sin reigned in death, so also grace might reign through righteousness to bring eternal life through Jesus Christ our Lord.*

In other words, the consequence of sin is death. As bad as sin leads to death is as good as God's grace leads to righteousness. You can't get any worse than sin that leads to death. On the flip side, you can't get any better in this life than God's grace, which brings eternal life through Jesus Christ! The hymn writer wrote it this way under the umbrella "Grace Greater Than Our Sins."

1. "Marvelous grace of our loving Lord,
Grace that exceeds our sin and our guilt!
Yonder on Calvary's mount outpoured,
There where the blood of the Lamb was spilled.

2. Dark is the stain that we cannot hide.
What can we do to wash it away?
Look! There is flowing a crimson tide,
Brighter than snow you may be today.

3. Marvelous, infinite, matchless grace,
Freely bestowed on all who believe!
You that are longing to see His face,
Will you this moment His grace receive?"

Chorus: Grace, Grace, God's Grace,
Grace that will pardon and cleanse within.
Grace, Grace, God's Grace,
Grace that is greater than all our sin.[1]

On my way home the other night, God revealed to me more about "Are we Following Jesus or Just Fooling Around" through the plight of a squirrel. On the road a mile from my house, a little squirrel ran out in front of me, and I saw up close the following scene of events. The squirrel screeched to a stop, started to run back, hesitated, looked back at me, turned as if to try to make it across to the other side, and at the last second, ran back safely from the side which he had first come. Aren't we just like that squirrel in our Christian life? We run out from God's grace and dangerously try to cross the road of an unforgiving nature towards others. We get scared and confused. If we continue across that unforgiving road, Satan will flatten us and defeat us. Yet, if we would just realize the error of our ways, God's grace will lead us safely home. We all need to run back to the cross and remember God's forgiveness and what it cost! When it is hard for you to forgive, listen closely to the voice of Jesus at Calvary:

> *" . . . Father, forgive them, for they do not know what they are doing. . ."*
> *(Luke 23:34)*

CHAPTER 3

"Faithfully Unfaithful"

CHAPTER TRUTH:

Christians are some of the most faithful people in the world! They are faithful to being unfaithful to God!

One of the most tragic events during the Reagan Presidency was the Sunday morning terrorist bombing of the Marine barracks in Beirut, in which hundreds of Americans were killed or wounded as they slept. Many of us can still recall the terrible scenes as the dazed survivors worked to dig out their trapped brothers from beneath the rubble.

A few days after the tragedy, I recall coming across an extraordinary story. Marine Corps Commandant Paul Kelly, visited some of the wounded survivors then in a Frankfurt, Germany, hospital. Among them was Corporal Jeffrey Lee Nashton, severely wounded in the incident. Nashton had so many tubes

*running in and out of his body that a
witness said he looked more like a
machine than a man; yet he survived.*

*As Kelly neared him, Nashton,
struggling to move and racked with
pain, motioned for a piece of paper
and a pen. He wrote a brief note and
passed it back to the Commandant. On
the slip of paper were but two words
— "Semper Fi" the Latin motto of the
Marines meaning "forever faithful."
With those two simple words Nashton
spoke for the millions of Americans
who have sacrificed body and limb
and their lives for their country —
those who have remained faithful.*[1]

"**S**emper Fi" – "Forever Faithful." It is a great
testimony that men and women have been so
faithful to their country that they would give up their
own lives. But it is a greater tragedy that men and
women have been, in so many ways, unfaithful to their
Christ who gave up His life so that we could live. Could
this possibly be one rare instance where it would do
good for the Christians to take a page out of the society's (marine's) playbook?! I believe we could all learn
a lot from marines about being faithful!!

Preachers all across the country sound "Lack of
Commitment" from God's pulpits. Yet, it is not a lack of
commitment. It is a lack of following Jesus and a lot of

fooling around. Christians today know how to make commitments. Christian people cannot commit to a 12-week course in Discipleship Training, but they can make BUNCO every Tuesday Night for 5 years! Christians cannot make it to Sunday School even two times a month, but they can take their children to school 5 days a week, 9 weeks a quarter, 9 months a year, for 9 straight years! Most Christians won't have one family devotion time in a whole year, but Sally, Suzie, and Steve won't miss one soccer practice, one band rehearsal, one gymnastics practice, or one Little League baseball game. Therefore, Christians don't lack commitment. We know how to make commitment to the things that are important to us. God just doesn't seem to be important enough for most Christians to be committed to Him.

A recent statistic that came across the radio airwaves stated, "There are presently over 4 Million Inactive Southern Baptist Church Members in America today." This means that over 4 million people expressed their faith in Jesus Christ and to His church, yet they are nowhere to be found when it comes to worshipping Christ. Many Christians are faithful to being unfaithful to God!

Imagine the scenario, which I have wished was only in my imagination, but have dealt with numerous times in real-life counseling situations. Your spouse of twenty years has been unfaithful to you. The one you have committed your life to and said "I do" to in front of God and witnesses, has committed adultery on you. Imagine your spouse said, "I cheated on you" in front of God, your family, and friends. Imagine the even more depressing situation that your spouse cheated on you with your best friend. Not only has your spouse cheated on you, betrayed your trust, and lied on his commitment to you, but also he was with another, emotionally and physically, that you introduced him to. Your spouse cheated on you with a person he would never have met or known if it had not been for you! How would you feel if your spouse was unfaithful to you? (The sad reality in our world today is that many of you reading this book don't have to imagine the situation, because you have all-to-painfully lived it!) Feelings of anger, resentment, betrayal, mistrust, loneliness, depression, and unloved all rolled-up into the ball of emotions entitled "UNFAITHFUL".

I wanted some of you to imagine, some of you to painfully re-live, unfaithfulness in hopes of shedding some light on how God must feel to those of us who often have been unfaithful to Him! We Christians are the Bride of Christ. And many times His Bride has been Unfaithful! How do you think Jesus feels when He died to give us life and we are more committed to the things of life than we are to the Giver of Life?! We wouldn't even know life if it wasn't for Jesus! Yet we have cheated on God by loving the things of this world more than the God who so loved this world that He sent His Son. Do you think Jesus feels betrayed?! Unloved?! Angry?! We know that one day Jesus will return, and He will handle in His way those who have been

Unfaithful! We read it in Revelation 19:

> *11 I saw heaven standing open and there before me was a white horse, **whose rider is called Faithful and True.** With justice he judges and makes war. 12 His eyes are like blazing fire, and on his head are many crowns. He has a name written on him that no one knows but he himself. 13 He is dressed in a robe dipped in blood, and his name is the Word of God. 14 The armies of heaven were following him, riding on white horses and dressed in fine linen, white and clean. 15 Out of his mouth comes a sharp sword with which to strike down the nations. "He will rule them with an iron scepter." He treads the winepress of the fury of the wrath of God Almighty. 16 On his robe and on his thigh he has this name written: KING OF KINGS AND LORD OF LORDS.* (Emphasis added by author)

He who is called "Faithful" will return one day to judge the unfaithful. Like many of you who have wanted to ring the neck of your betrayer and his mistress, Jesus will one day "tread the winepress of the fury of the wrath of God Almighty." May we, His Bride, realize how unfaithful we have been and return to our first love!

I believe many of our unfaithful times in life stem from our cravings to be successful. The rat race of life has caused many to rat out on their love-relationship with God.

> *Mark Hatfield tells of touring Calcutta with Mother Teresa and visiting the so-called "House of Dying," where sick children are cared for in their last days, and the dispensary, where the poor line up by the hundreds to receive medical attention. Watching Mother Teresa minister to these people, feeding and nursing those left by others to die, Hatfield was overwhelmed by the sheer magnitude of the suffering she and her co-workers face daily. "How can you bear the load without being crushed by it?" he asked. Mother Teresa replied, "My dear Senator, I am not called to be successful, I am called to be faithful."* 2

I don't know about you, but I need the daily reminder that "I am not called to be successful, I am called to be faithful!"

The problem of "Faithfully Unfaithful" finds its basis in the question, "Why can't we be Faithful to the One who is always faithful to us?" For me, the answer involves misplaced perspectives. God's Word says in

Hebrews:

> *13:5 Keep your lives free from the love
> of money and be content with what
> you have, because God has said,
> "Never will I leave you;
> never will I forsake you."
> 6 So we say with confidence,
> "The Lord is my helper; I will not be
> afraid.
> What can man do to me?"*

You see, sometimes we lose perspective on what really matters in life. It doesn't matter what the world tries to do to me; it only matters who God is to me! It does not matter how much money I obtain; it only matters how much of me the Master holds! What matters most is He who has always been Faithful to me!

Poor circumstances often lead to a poor perspective on life. Many times when life does not go our way, we turn our focus from our Prince of Peace to our problems or our pain. Next time you are tempted to fool around in your faithfulness and not follow Jesus, maybe this next story will keep you in His footsteps no matter what situation you may encounter.

> *An elderly preacher was rebuked by
> one of his deacons one Sunday morn-
> ing before the service. "Pastor," said
> the man, "something must be wrong*

with your preaching and your work. There's been only one person added to the church in a whole year, and he's just a boy." The minister listened, his eyes moistening and his thin hand trembling. "I feel it all," he replied, "but God knows I've tried to do my duty." On that day the minister's heart was heavy as he stood before his flock. As he finished the message, he felt a strong inclination to resign. After everyone else had left, that one boy came to him and asked, "Do you think if I worked hard for an education, I could become a preacher—perhaps a missionary?" Again tears welled up in the minister's eyes. "Ah, this heals the ache I feel," he said. "Robert, I see the Divine hand now. May God bless you, my boy. Yes, I think you will become a preacher." Many years later an aged missionary returned to London from Africa. His name was spoken with reverence. Nobles invited him to their homes. He had added many souls to the church of Jesus Christ, reaching even some of Africa's most savage chiefs. His name was Robert Moffat, the same Robert who years before had spoken to the pastor that Sunday morning in the old Scottish Kirk.[3]

"Lord, help us to be faithful. Then give us the grace to leave the results to You!"

I am so glad that Jesus is Faithfully Faithful. His Word says over and over again that He is Faithful!

1 Corinthians 1:9

> *9 God, who has called you into fellowship with his Son Jesus Christ our Lord, is faithful.*

1 Corinthians 10:13

> *13 And God is faithful; he will not let you be tempted beyond what you can bear. But when you are tempted, he will also provide a way out so that you can stand up under it.*

2 Timothy 2:13

> *13 If we are faithless, he will remain faithful, for he cannot disown himself..*

Hebrews 3:6

> *6 But Christ is faithful as a son over God's house. And we are his house, if we hold on to our courage and the hope of which we boast.*

They say that "Semper Fi" is a Latin motto. But I

believe that "Forever Faithful" originated as the Lord's motto! God's Word is faithful to continually express the faithfulness of God.

Deuteronomy 7:9

> *9 Know therefore that the LORD your God is God; he is the faithful God, keeping his covenant of love to a thousand generations of those who love him and keep his commands.*

2 Samuel 22:26-28

> *26 "To the faithful you show yourself faithful, to the blameless you show yourself blameless, 27 to the pure you show yourself pure, but to the crooked you show yourself shrewd. 28 You save the humble, but your eyes are on the haughty to bring them low.*

And what happens to those who quit fooling around and really start following Jesus? What will the Lord say to those who remain faithful to the One who is Faithful and True?

> *23 "His master replied, **'Well done, good and faithful servant!** You have been faithful with a few things; I will put you in charge of many things. Come and share your master's happiness!' "*

Matthew 25:23
(Emphasis added by author)

A Pause
For
Perspective

I feel like God would have me to pause between these two chapters to articulate what God just laid on my heart. A few people have read what has been written thus far and have made some encouraging comments. Some of those comments are, "People can think of certain individuals from your analogies." And "This book will keep people interested as they can automatically think of people they know that fit certain descriptions." While it is encouraging that readers can relate, and I gather what they mean, the goal of this book is to help you (the reader) to start following Jesus and stop fooling around. So rather than thinking about how your friends and family need to read this book, read this book and let God deal with you. (Then, afterwards, go and buy a copy for your family and friends! All proceeds will go to help children in Mississippi. Namely, both of mine!!)

But seriously, I'm writing this book *NOT* to make

money, but because I desperately need to quit fooling around and to start following Jesus! Tonight, as I am beginning to write Chapter 4 – "Genuinely Hypocritical", I am reminded by My Redeemer how I have to write this book and allow God to deal with me, just as you have to read this book and let God deal with you. Amanda and I got in a rather large disagreement tonight over something insignificant. Her emotions escalated directly proportional to my spiritual gift of "egging-on" (I mean ability). Then, Amanda, knowing what chapter I was beginning to write, said (yelled) "You are writing 'Genuinely Hypocritical' and you are the biggest hypocrite I know!" As I write these words on a yellow steno pad, I am leaning forward in my glider rocker so that the existing dagger will not go any deeper! OUCH!! God has a way of using pain to point out the principle of perspective. Your closest friends and family see you for who you are better than you are willing to admit to yourself. So as I write this next chapter through the anointing of the Holy Spirit, realize that this, and every chapter, preaches first of all to the stabbed heart behind this pen. You, the reader, allow God to deal with it in your heart as He best sees fit! May God bless your journey towards following Jesus!

CHAPTER 4

"Genuinely Hypocritical"

CHAPTER TRUTH:

Christians are not very good at being hypocrites. You would think if you were a hypocrite, that you could at least hide it!

Webster defines "Hypocrisy" from the Greek *hypokrisis* – "*Acting a part*" and from *hypokrinesthai* – "*to play a part, pretend.*" This dictionary continues to define "hypocrisy" as "*the acting of a false part; a deception as to real character and feeling, especially in regard to morals and religion.*" Webster then defines the word "hypocrite" as follows: "*A pretender. One who feigns to be what he is not; especially one who pretends to be pious, virtuous, etc. without really being so.*" The adverb "hypocritely" is defined as "*deceptively.*"[1] I particularly like the following definition of hypocrite: "A hypocrite can be defined as someone who complains that there is too much sex and violence on his VCR."[2]

Who better to write about "acting out of a false part" than a preacher who has a twin brother?! All my life, Ricky and I have been trading places and fooling people. The following true stories are mentioned just to name a few and to let you know how far I have come with the Lord since then:

- The first major deception occurred in 5th grade. Ricky and I had the same class schedule except that I had English 2nd period and Social Studies 5th period and Ricky had Social Studies 2nd period and English 5th period. (The temptation was put in place by the school system and their scheduling!) Anyway, the inevitable happened. We had an English test and Social Studies test on the same day. You guessed it! Ricky took the English test twice, and I took the Social Studies test twice! It would have worked if I had not signed my name to both Social Studies tests. (My Doctorate was earned at a later date, with no help from Ricky!!)

- From the day they caught us (or I was a dunce and caught myself), the school system forced us to take the same schedule of classes through high school graduation. Not to be outsmarted by the school system, another opportunity arose! Our senior year, our Calculus teacher gave us a test on two chapters every time. She would have one page on one chapter and one page on another. So Ricky would study one chapter and I would study the other. During test time, Ricky would answer the page he had studied, and I would do the same. Then we would give the signal (scratch the right eyebrow), and we would both head to the pencil sharpener at the front of class. Afterward, we would go back to the other's desk and fill out the page we knew. This was never caught by the teacher. But it did catch up with us in college when Ricky only knew the odd chapters and I only knew the even ones!!

- This deceptive nature as twins also showed up in athletics. When we were juniors in high school, both of us played on the baseball team. Ricky was a backup shortstop, and I was, supposedly, going to start left field that season. The week before the baseball season started, we both went on a Beta Club Convention trip to the Mississippi Gulf Coast. I stepped on a piece of glass on the beach and had 18 stitches put in the bottom of my right foot. So, as we put our two heads together, Ricky and I decided that it would be ridiculous for both of us to be benchwarmers. Therefore, Ricky posed as me and started left field. The problem was that by the time the coach discovered the deception, Ricky was doing so well that I never did get my position back when I fully recovered!

- Probably the deception that took the grand prize occurred our sophomore year in high school. Two senior girls asked Ricky and I to the Jr./Sr. prom. They were really nice girls, but not our girlfriends – just good friends. We double-dated which is appropriate for twins don't you think? Ricky wore a white tux, blue cummerbund, and bow tie; while I wore a white tux with a black cummerbund and bow tie. (You can already see where this is going.) About halfway through the dance, Ricky whispered into my ear, "Come with me to the bathroom." (I thought only girls did that, but twins do it too!) Anyway, Ricky and I switched cummerbunds and bow ties, and our dates never knew the difference. (I thought that mine would, because I dance so much better than Ricky! Oh, I can't say that – I am a Baptist preacher!!) Well, he walked my date to the door of her house, and I walked his date back to her door. On the way home, I made sure that he didn't kiss my date!!

- Ricky and I currently serve on staff together. And often, Senior Adult ladies will tell Ricky how much they enjoyed his sermon when I preach. Maybe they just really want me to let him preach more!

Therefore, I know a lot about masquerading as someone that I am not.

I've also learned first hand about hypocrisy in eight years of student ministry. One time I saw some of my youth in a car, so I drove up next to them in my truck. I could see smoke filling up their car and knew that the Marlboro Man was not in the back seat. When they saw it was me, they all put their hands down behind their seats holding on to the smoking cigarette. I acted like I was blind and said, "What are ya'll doing tonight?" And they (no lie – no deception at all. The honest truth) said, "Oh, we are just going to go and hand out some gospel tracts." I just played along and made up things to keep them talking. They kept saying, "Well, we have got to go." And I kept saying, "What's your hurry? Stay and talk to me for a while." All the while I was praying, "God let it burn their hand, just a little, and teach them a lesson!"

Did you notice in Webster's definition of hypocrisy the part that read: *a deception as to real character and feeling, especially in regard to morals and religion.*[3] Even Webster associates hypocrisy with the church!! Has it gotten so bad that many of us Christians are "genuinely hypocritical"? "George Barna's research showed that ¾ of Americans thinks it is important for people to read the Bible, but only 13% actually read the Bible daily." [4]

Although some people think that the church has the exclusive rights to play-actors, a couple of true stories might lend a different perspective.

- A St. Louis prosecutor spearheaded a crusade against prostitution and pornography. This man led a crackdown on the rental of adult movies at video stores and was a strong supporter of a sting operation to prevent prostitution. But in 1992, this same prosecutor was charged with soliciting an undercover police officer posing as a prostitute at the St. Louis Airport Marriot Hotel.[5]

• The head of the Internal Revenue Service from 1961-1964, after much resistance, finally agreed to pay $308,408 in back taxes for his federal income taxes from 1980-1982. [6]

Whether we like it or not, the world we live in is full of hypocrites. Just note the following story:

> *Drs. Hillel Finestone and David Conter, of the University of Western Ontario, think medical doctors should take acting classes so they can at least pretend they are concerned about their patients. These two doctors are not being facetious. They have written their thoughts for the medical community to seriously consider. "We do not put forward the idea cynically," they said. These physicians feel "acting classes should be required in medical school so doctors can learn just when to provide a perfectly timed compassionate look, or a touch on the hand." An accompanying commentary from Great Britain by Dr. Chris McManus of St. Mary's Hospital Medical School in London said, "acting may ultimately save doctors who are at risk of profes-*

sional burnout." [7]

I guess that these doctors feel like authentic compassion would have to require authentic concern that they don't have. I tell you, Christians ought to be concerned about this. There are far too many Christians just fooling around and only pretending and play-acting as if they are really following Jesus!

But all this hypocrisy is nothing new to the world we live in. Hollywood has been playing pretend for a long time now. On most sets in Hollywood, cameras and actors lead people to believe they are in a huge city, when in reality, they are only in front of a cardboard stage. In every Hollywood movie, the good guy lives, the bad guy gets caught, and the ugly, scrawny guy wins the heart of Miss Gorgeous. (Oh, by the way, Miss Gorgeous is not usually, in reality, beautiful until after her fifth plastic surgery!) Hollywood is genuinely artificial and hilariously hypocritical! On the other hand, everything that happened on Holy Wood 2000 years ago is really real and Genuinely GOD!

Jesus was really real. In fact, He never played a role. He pursued the Righteous life that His Heavenly Father desired for Him. And often in Scripture, Jesus revealed His genuineness: One example is John 6:53-59:

> *53 Jesus said to them, "I tell you the truth, unless you eat the flesh of the Son of Man and drink his blood, you have no life in you. 54 Whoever eats*

*my flesh and drinks my blood has eternal life, and I will raise him up at the last day. 55 For my flesh is **real** food and my blood is **real** drink. 56 Whoever eats my flesh and drinks my blood remains in me, and I in him. 57 Just as the living Father sent me and I live because of the Father, so the one who feeds on me will live because of me. 58 This is the bread that came down from heaven. Your forefathers ate manna and died, but he who feeds on this bread will live forever." 59 He said this while teaching in the synagogue in Capernaum.* (Emphasis added by author)

So while teaching in the temple, Jesus let everyone know that His blood spilt and body striped was the real thing. Everything about Calvary screams that Jesus was Really Real! From the sacrifice to the suffering, from the love to the forgiveness, everything about Golgotha was real. You don't get anymore real than the cross, and you don't get anything more relevant than the empty tomb!

If Jesus is really real, then why is it that so many of His followers are so genuinely artificial?! Jesus addressed this often in His Word to those who supposedly knew His Word, yet who had major problems applying it to their lives.

Matthew 23:24-28

24 You blind guides! You strain out a gnat but swallow a camel.

25 "Woe to you, teachers of the law and Pharisees, you hypocrites! You clean the outside of the cup and dish, but inside they are full of greed and self-indulgence. 26 Blind Pharisee! First clean the inside of the cup and dish, and then the outside also will be clean.

27 "Woe to you, teachers of the law and Pharisees, you hypocrites! You are like whitewashed tombs, which look beautiful on the outside but on the inside are full of dead men's bones and everything unclean. 28 In the same way, on the outside you appear to people as righteous but on the inside you are full of hypocrisy and wickedness.

Matthew 16:6

6 "Be careful," Jesus said to them. "Be on your guard against the yeast of the Pharisees and Sadducees."

There has been a lot of yeast spread throughout the church in the area of Christians that are genuinely hypocritical. There has been a lot of fooling around when it comes to this issue and very little true following of Jesus.

For goodness sake, (or more importantly, for the sake of God), if Hollywood can fake it and fool people, why, you would think that Christians could at least be good actors?! But we aren't good pretenders. Ricky and I always got caught! If not by teachers, coaches, or parents; we got caught by the consequences of our actions. And our All-knowing God knows all of us who are hypocrites in His Kingdom. You better realize that He who is Really Real knows how to spot an artificial follower!

I will close this chapter on Genuinely Hypocritical, while I seek to one day close this chapter in my life of fooling around in my relationship to my Real Redeemer. Note the following in conclusion:

> *Steve Green is a very successful Christian vocalist who has also succeeded in writing. In his book, **Listening Heart**, he shares some insightful truths. Although he has a passion for holiness, he recognizes within his own life the tendency we all have of occasionally being dishonest spiritually. To remind himself of this tendency to become hypocritical, he says, "I am still a recovering hypocrite." Although we quickly become defensive when someone says*

*the church is full of hypocrites, we
would do better to acknowledge that
we are all "recovering hypocrites"
who could very easily slip back into
the sin of hypocrisy.* [8]

May we all pray for each other, so that we can do more
following Jesus and less fooling around!!

CHAPTER 5

"Happily Unjoyful"

CHAPTER TRUTH:

Many Christians love throwing a party – a pity party or a bash of bitterness. Don't ever ask these people, "How are you doing?" unless you just want them to lie and answer, "Fine."

＋≈≈≒＋

How can those of us who have found real joy in Jesus display a lack of joy in our spiritual lives? If you stood on any given sanctuary platform on any given Sunday, you would find several sad and pitiful looking faces supposedly worshiping the God of all Joy and Peace! They sing "Amazing Grace" while they are amazingly grieved! They sing "Joyful, Joyful We Adore Thee", but their faces scream "Woeful, Woeful, Oh Anguished Me." Often at Christmas we sing, "Joy to the World! The Lord Is Come" while inwardly for many, what really has come is the selfishness and hurried pace of the Christmas season! Can those who have the God of Joy living in their lives truly ever lose this joy? Not in a million years - better yet, not in all eternity!

Churchgoers aren't the only ones who seem to have trouble tapping into their joy in Jesus. Ministers for the Good News many times focus on nothing but the bad news. The following exemplifies this:

> *Oliver Wendell Holmes, Jr., was a member of the U.S. Supreme Court for 30 years. His mind, wit, and work earned him the unofficial title of "the greatest justice since John Marshall." At one point in his life, Justice Holmes explained his choice of a career by saying: "I might have entered the ministry if certain clergymen I knew had not looked and acted so much like undertakers."* [1]

What a sad testimony towards those who share the path to real joy in life!

So there are Christian churchgoers and Christian preachers who have found joy in Jesus, and yet, people very rarely find joy in them. And all the while Jesus says in John 10:10, *"The thief comes only to steal and kill and destroy; I have come that they may have life, and have it to the full."* Where is that full life? What are the joy stealers that seek to withdraw from the joy bank account of the redeemed?

The first and foremost robber of joy is bitterness. Webster defines "bitter" as *"mournful, distressing; expressive of misery."* Webster then defines "bitterness" as *"the state or quality of being bitter; deep distress of mind."* [2] That is exactly how so many Christians are. They are distressed over some situation in the past, and they have allowed it to cause a deep distress of their minds. Note the following story:

One day, two monks were walking through the countryside. They were on their way to another village to help bring in the crops. As they walked, they spied an old woman sitting at the edge of a river. She was upset because there was no bridge, and she could not get across on her own. The first monk kindly offered, "We will carry you across if you would like." "Thank you," she said gratefully, accepting their help. So the two men joined hands, lifted her between them and carried her across the river. When they got to the other side, they set her down, and she went on her way. After they had walked another mile or so, the second monk began to complain. "Look at my clothes," he said. "They are filthy from carrying that woman across the river. And my back still hurts from lifting her. I can feel it getting stiff." The first monk just smiled and nodded his head. A few more miles up the road, the second monk griped again, "My back is hurting me so badly, and it is all because we had to carry that silly woman across the river! I cannot go any farther because of the pain." The first monk looked down at his partner, now lying on the ground, moaning. "Have you wondered why I am not complaining?" he asked. "Your back hurts because you are still carrying the woman. But I set her down five miles ago."

That is what many of us are like in dealing with our families. We are that second monk who cannot let go. We hold the pain of the past over our loved ones' heads like a club, or we remind them every once in a while, when we want to get the upper hand, of the burden we still carry because of something they did years ago. ³

Until we are ready to lay down the burden that has caused us distress and duress, the thief that comes to steal will continue to rob us of joy.

A second robber of the joy-filled life is complaining. Webster defines "complaining" as *"to utter expressions of grief, pain, or dissatisfaction."*⁴ Thus, if bitterness is not broken, complaining will continue to be expressed! All of us know people who are constantly looking for something to complain about. They think that complaining is a spiritual gift, but it is a present that most of us wish was never opened! The following quote expresses the art of complaining well.

> *"Think about the oyster. It takes a grain of sand and turns it into a beautiful pearl. Too often we are just the opposite—we take pearls and turn them into grains of sand."*[5]

All too often, we will take the gift of eternal and abundant life and exchange it for eternal bitterness and an abundance of complaints.

Also, many of those who complain do so because it allows them not to notice <u>their</u> faults and failures. They seem to think that if they find faults in others, then their own failures are not so bad. Another quote says it best:

> *"You will find that, as a rule, those who complain about the way the ball bounces are usually the ones who dropped it."* [6]

Complaining allows one to focus outward, drawing attention away from the scarred soul of the one doing the complaining. All the while, the issues of the heart are ignored, and the pains compounded as bitterness increase proportionally to the complaints.

A third thief of joy is comparison. When Satan can't make you bitter enough to complain, he will seek to lower your self-esteem and allow you to compare. And then, those who supposedly are living the abundant life start throwing an abundance of pity parties. So when you sit down and cater a pity party for yourselves about how you just aren't important to the kingdom, because you can't do this or that, don't expect Jesus to attend as a sympathetic guest. The only association Jesus has with pity parties is—He crashes them with the truth. He is the quintessential pity-party crasher. He comes in with his **God**-centeredness and throws cold water on us. He tells us to stop thinking about how we aren't like other people and don't have what others have. Our job is not to look at other people and compare ourselves with them, but to look to Him and get our value and worth from Him. The reason we should do that is because GOD has designed us, and He doesn't make mistakes. When we whine to God, we are telling the Omniscient, Almighty, Master Designer of all creation that He really goofed, because He didn't give this to us or didn't make us more like that other person.

There are so many ways that the thief comes in to steal, kill, and destroy the abundant life of the believer. Bitterness, complaining, and comparison all stem from the root problem of selfishness. Satan can only steal your joy if you are self-centered rather than gazing on God. When you focus on Jesus and consider Him, the joy flows.

> *2 Let us fix our eyes on Jesus, the*
> *author and perfecter of our faith,* **who**
> **for the joy set before him endured the**

cross, scorning its shame, and sat down at the right hand of the throne of God. 3 Consider him who endured such opposition from sinful men, so that you will not grow weary and lose heart. (Hebrews 12:2-3). [Emphasis added by author]

When you get God-directed, you realize that <u>you</u> were the joy set before Jesus on the cross of Calvary! That will bring joy to your soul!! When you look at Jesus, you realize that with nails in hands and feet, while breathing His last breath in searing pain, joy filled His heart! Joy? Yes, Joy! Joy because Jesus knew that through His death, we would be able one day to receive life! Jesus knew that through His pain, we would be able to receive peace! Jesus endured the jeers of the crowd, so that we could encounter the joy of Christ. Jesus suffered the beating, so that we could be served a blessing! Jesus was beat beyond recognition, so that we could be recognized as His Children! Jesus was hung up for our hang-ups, so that we could one day be called up! He who knew no sin became sin for us, so that we could know no death! When you consider Him, you can be filled with joy no matter what you are going through!! Whatever is happening in your life, Jesus will make a way through to the other side.

13 No temptation has seized you except what is common to man. And God is faithful; he will not let you be tempted beyond what you can bear. But when you are tempted, he will also provide a way out so that you can stand up under it. (1 Corinthians 10:13)

The key to living a joy-filled life is following Jesus! If you are just fooling around, you will never have the faith-focus that will bring you daily joy!

Those who really followed Jesus in Scripture found joy in the midst of excruciating situations. Focus on the following, and you will see those who discovered joy:

- The people of God during the rebuilding of their tabernacle.
  "Do not grieve, for the joy of the LORD is your strength."
  (Nehemiah 8:10)

- The women at the empty tomb found joy amidst their fear.
  "So the women hurried away from the tomb, afraid yet filled with joy, and ran to tell his disciples." (Matthew 28:8)

- Paul found joy in the midst of his troubles.
  "I have great confidence in you; I take great pride in you. I am greatly encouraged; in all our troubles my joy knows no bounds."

(2 Corinthians 7:3-4)

• The Macedonian churches found joy through trials and poverty.
"Out of the most severe trial, their overflowing joy and their extreme poverty welled up in rich generosity." (2 Corinthians 8:2)

When you stop fooling around and really start following Jesus, joy abounds in all circumstances and situations of life.

> *"As a third-century man was anticipating death, he penned these last words to a friend: 'It's a bad world, an incredibly bad world. But I have discovered in the midst of it a quiet and holy people who have learned a great secret. They have found a joy which is a thousand times better than any pleasure of our sinful life. They are despised and persecuted, but they care not. They are masters of their souls. They have overcome the world. These people are the Christians—and I am one of them.'"* [7]

It is those people who truly follow Jesus that will find a true joy that this world will never, ever, be able to take away.

Those that are following Jesus are enjoying the journey realizing that pain brings progress and challenges build character.

> *2 Consider it pure joy, my brothers, whenever you face trials of many kinds, 3 because you know that the testing of your faith develops perseverance. 4 Perseverance must finish its work so that you may be mature and complete, not lacking anything. (James 1:2-4)*

When you focus on the fact that God is making you in His own likeness, the pity party turns into a passionate walk with your Savior!

The joy robber hates it when you find joy in Jesus in any and every circumstance of life. The devil makes a fool of those who are fooling around in their walk with the Lord. But the devil is made a fool when you really start following your Savior.

The key to living with joy is abiding in Jesus. That is why after His discourse on abiding (the word is used eleven times in the first ten verses), Jesus says:

> *10 If you obey my commands, you will remain in my love, just as I have obeyed my Father's commands and remain in his love. 11 **I have told you this so that my joy may be in you and***

that your joy may be complete.
(John 15:10-11) [Emphasis added by
Author]

Christ died on the cross so that you could find complete
joy in ***Jesus***!

Fool around with your spiritual life and you will miss
real ***joy***!

Follow ***Jesus*** and you will find ***Joy*** in the Journey!

Another
Pause
For
Perspective

‐‑‐

If you are trying to lead your own life, you will never truly be able to follow Jesus. This is revealed in the following story.

> *S. I. McMillen, in his book <u>None of These Diseases</u>, tells a story of a young woman who wanted to go to college, but her heart sank when she read the question on the application blank that asked, "Are you a leader?" Being both honest and conscientious, she wrote, "No," and returned the application, expecting the worst. To her surprise, she received this letter from the college: "Dear Applicant: A study of the application forms reveals that this year our college will have 1,452 new leaders. We are accepting*

*you because we feel it is imperative
that they have at least one follower."* [1]

Many times in the projects of life, we have too many
chiefs and two few Indians. Everybody wants to be a
leader. There are a million books out there today on
how to develop your leadership skills. But there are too
few works on how to develop your skills as a follower.

Jesus is The Leader for all leaders and Chief of all
chiefs. Jesus doesn't need more leaders nearly as bad as
He desires more followers. You will never lead until
you truly learn to follow. And who better to follow than
Jesus!

CHAPTER 6

"Evangelistically Un-evangelistic"

CHAPTER TRUTH:

Christians are some of the most evangelistic people I know. The only problem is they do a bad job of spreading the Good News and a good job of spreading the bad news!

I do not know who coined the phrase "Good news travels fast." But if good news travels fast, it seems that in our world, bad news travels faster! If you want to get something on the 10:00 o-clock news, make it bad news. Editors will tell you that somebody building a house for a homeless man or cleaning up the yard for the elderly is not newsworthy. But let a man attack a dog or his wife and kids, and those same editors call that "Front-Page News." That is why "Shock Radio", "Day-time soaps", "Talk-shows", and television programs like "Law and Order" are so popular. They all center on the bad things that happen in our world. (When is the last time you saw a daytime soap that had nothing but good news on for a half-hour?) We live in a sin-sick world that craves for the weird, outrageous, ugly, and perverted.

It seems that Christians have followed suit with the ways of the world. Some would rather spread bad news than the Gospel (Good News) of Jesus Christ! The following true story illustrates this fact:

> *The Times-Reporter of New Philadelphia, Ohio, reported in September 1985 a celebration of a New Orleans municipal pool. The party around the pool was held to celebrate the first summer in memory without a drowning at the New Orleans city pool. In honor of the occasion, 200 people gathered, including 100 certified lifeguards. As the party was breaking up and the four lifeguards on duty began to clear the pool, they found a fully dressed body in the deep end. They tried to revive Jerome Moody, 31, but it was too late. He had drowned surrounded by lifeguards celebrating their successful season.*[1]

Could that describe the Church of Jesus Christ today? Are we celebrating a successful season because we had fifty people who moved their church membership from another church to "our" church? While in the same year, people are dying all around our churches lost without Christ! Do we spread gossip more than we share the Good News?

Well, maybe a closer look at Wednesday night Prayer meetings will shed some more light on this subject. How many prayer requests on Wednesday nights are for people who have had bad things happen to them? It appears at times that some people try to out bad news the person sitting to their left. Maybe a similar conversation has happened during your weekly prayer services.

> Church Member: *Pastor, could you please pray for my Uncle's third cousin's father? He fell off the roof of a house, broke both legs and sprained his right wrist. And when he tried to get up, not knowing his legs were broken, he fell on his face and chipped three of his teeth. Now he has to get porcelain veneers. And he lost his job the week before, that's why he got the odd job on the roof, and he can't afford porcelain veneers. So please pray for him.*
> Pastor: *What is his name?*
> Church Member: *Oh, I don't know his name.*

Are we trying to come up with the worst-case scenario in our prayer meetings? Is there some imaginary, invisible trophy passed each week to the member who tops all others? Then, try to ask for "Praise Items" and everyone who had a sick brother or cousin shuts up tighter than a Finance Committee chairman during budget increase time! This just doesn't make any sense to me!

People desire to share good news in other areas of their lives as long as there is not a catch somewhere. For example, I haven't met a couple trying to have children that didn't want to shout it from the rooftops when the lady got pregnant. However, a couple out of wedlock would try to hide the fact that the woman was pregnant. I don't know a single man who would not tell all his buddies when he found "Miss Right." But I don't know one man who would tell all his friends he found "Miss Right" if he was already married to another Mrs. You see, when there is a catch, people don't spread news as good news. But there is no catch at all to the Good News of the Gospel of Jesus Christ. We were lost and now we are found! We were imprisoned by sin, and now we can be set free by grace through faith! What price we couldn't pay, Jesus sacrificed His life for and paid in full, signed with His own blood! No catch! Nothing but pure Good News!

So why would we spend our time in churches planning on sharing the Good News more than practicing sharing the gospel? Christians talk more about how to do evangelism, than they actually evangelize. For example:

> *While D.L. Moody was attending a convention in Indianapolis on mass evangelism, he asked his song leader Ira Sankey to meet him at 6 o'clock one evening at a certain street corner.*

*When Sankey arrived, Mr. Moody
asked him to stand on a box and sing.
Once a crowd had gathered, Moody
spoke briefly and then invited the
people to follow him to the nearby
convention hall. Soon the auditorium
was filled with spiritually hungry
people, and the great evangelist
preached the gospel to them. Then the
convention delegates began to arrive.
Moody stopped preaching and said,
"Now we must close, as the brethren
of the convention wish to come and
discuss the topic, 'How to reach the
masses.'" Moody graphically illus-
trated the difference between talking
about doing something and going out
and doing it.* [2]

When it comes to evangelism, we need to follow the
Greek admonition for victory *"Nike"* and *"Just do it!"*

Do we evangelicals really practice evangelism?
How could you tell if we actually evangelize the lost as
much as we claim to do?

*It is easy to determine when something
is aflame. It ignites other material.
Any fire that does not spread will
eventually go out. A church without
evangelism is a contradiction in terms,*

> *just as a fire that does not burn is a contradiction.* [3]

If we are on fire for Jesus evangelistically, then those fires for Jesus ought to be spreading like wildfire. Yes, we do see churches experiencing revival! But are we encountering enough evangelism to really call ourselves evangelicals? (I can't point a finger at anyone but myself, so I will let you answer that question for yourself!)

If we are to actually evangelize the world, what actually does "evangelism" mean? J.I. Packer expresses this about evangelism:

> *Evangelism includes the endeavor to elicit a response to the truth taught. It is communication with a view to conversion. It is a matter, not merely of informing, but also of inviting.*[4]

So real evangelism has not occurred just because we have informed lost people on how to be saved. Good News needs to be expressed, but there must come a point of invitation for Good News to be experienced!

When it comes to evangelism, we desperately need to follow Jesus. We need to heed to the Word of God.

1 Be imitators of God, therefore, as dearly loved children 2 and live a life of love, just as Christ loved us and gave himself up for us as a fragrant offering and sacri-

fice to God. (Ephesians 5:1-2)
Jesus was a true evangelist. His purpose and mission in life was to tell the Good News of salvation.

43 But he (Jesus) said, "I must preach the good news of the kingdom of God to the other towns also, because that is why I was sent." (Luke 4:43)
The reason Jesus was sent was to preach the Good News! And so, that ought to be our purpose in life also. Those are not my words, but His!

21 Again Jesus said, "Peace be with you! As the Father has sent me, I am sending you." (John 20:21)
And Jesus didn't hide the Good News. He publicly expressed it in words and deed. This is expressed vividly in an excerpt from a poem with an anonymous author:

> " . . . *Jesus was not crucified in a cathedral between two candles;*
> *But on a cross between two thieves: on a town garbage heap; at a crossroad of politics so cosmopolitan that they had to write His title in Hebrew and in Latin and in Greek. . ."*[5]

We can't hide the Good News from a world that so desperately needs it!

"To withhold a medical remedy from

the sick, to withhold warning of fire from those in a burning building, to withhold critical evidence in a court of law – these are criminal offenses. To withhold the Good News from those who so desperately need it is a terrible sin. Sharing the Good News of Christ must be our priority!"[6]

What greater purpose in life could there be but to tell a world full of bad news that there is Good News found in Jesus!?

In order not to do what happens often in the realm of Christianity today, this chapter will be one of the shortest in the book. Personally, I don't wish to *talk* more about evangelism. I desperately desire to *do* more sharing the Good News. So I close with the following motivation.

The young salesman was disappointed about losing a big sale, and as he talked with his sales manager he lamented, "I guess it just proves you can lead a horse to water but you can't make him drink." The manager replied, "Son, take my advice: your job is not to make him drink. Your job is to make him thirsty." So it is with evangelism. Our lives should be so filled with Christ that they create a thirst for the Gospel.[7]

So let's all quit fooling around and start following Jesus!

CHAPTER 7

"Competitively Noncompetitive"

CHAPTER TRUTH:

We are so competitive within the Kingdom of God that we cannot compete with the united forces of evil in this world.

N obody likes a loser. You have to compete to win. But in order to win you have to fight the opposing team and not fight within your team.

"It was a dark and dreary day in 1916, a day well suited to the most brutally devastating rout in all of football history. One look at the two teams showed trouble ahead. On the Georgia Tech side were semi-human monsters, gorilla-like behemoths trained by John Heisman, the man football's highest award was later named after. Heisman was a fanatic. He would not let his Yellow Jackets use soap or water because he considered them debilitating. Nor could they eat pastry, pork, veal, hot bread, nuts, apples, or coffee.

His reason? "They don't agree with me," he growled, "so they'd better not agree with you." The Yellow Jackets, with eight All-Southern players, were intent on building their reputation. They lured lowly Cumberland to the game with a $500 guarantee. The Cumberland team had several players who had never played football before. The official who accepted the offer had long since graduated and left the team in the hands of the team manager. Even the trip to Atlanta had been a disaster: Cumberland arrived with only 16 players. Three were lost at a rest stop in Nashville. The game began. Georgia Tech scored 63 points in the first quarter, averaging touchdowns at one-minute-and-twenty-second intervals. Even after such a lopsided start, the rest of the game was filled with tension and drama! No one questioned who would win, of course. But could Cumberland players be convinced to finish the game? The manager, George Allen, paced the sidelines, exhorting the team to "hang in there for Cumberland's $500." They did, and with it collected the honor of the worst loss in college football *history: 222-0.*

One play must be mentioned. A Cumberland kickoff returner fumbled, probably from sheer weariness. He yelled to a teammate, "Pick up the ball!" Replied his teammate, "Pick it up yourself! You dropped it!" [1]

As Christians, we have dropped the ball when it comes to fighting the devil – our archrival. We are fighting with each other over which aquarium the fish will swim in rather than fishing for men, women, and children who are spiritually outside the aquarium and need life-giving water!

Competition can sometimes be quite humorous as the following story proves:

April 5, 1979. A Midwest Burger King was robbed last night. Police have arrested . . . are you ready for this? Burger King was robbed last night and police have arrested eighteen-year-old Ronald McDonald. [2]

Now that is what I call really robbing from the competition. While there are humorous incidences of competition, there is nothing funny about Christians fighting Christians and churches fighting against churches!

Webster defines "compete" as "to seek or strive for the same things as another" or "to strive in opposition."[3] One church gets jealous when another church thrives and is blessed. Why can't we be excited that God is building His Kingdom? We are not in opposition with each other. Other churches are not the competition; Satan and the evil forces of this world are! How could we lose sight of our common goal? How could we be focused on what other churches or denominations are doing rather than on the daily battle that we are in with temptation and the world? We have lost our focus! When it comes to competition, we are fooling around. And the only fool is the one who is in ministry for "their church" and not "God's Kingdom."

> *In a Peanuts cartoon Lucy demanded that Linus change TV channels, threatening him with her fist if he didn't. "What makes you think you can walk right in here and take over?" asks Linus. "These five fingers," says Lucy. "Individually they're nothing but when I curl them together like this into a single unit, they form a weapon that is terrible to behold." "Which channel do you want?" asks Linus. Turning away, he looks at his fingers and says, "Why can't you guys get organized like that?"* [4]

Why can't Christians get together and fight together the evils of this world rather than fighting with each other?

Competition runs in our veins. Why else would a father beat and kill a man cheering for the opposing team at a youth Hockey game? Why would a brawl break out between parents at a Little League Baseball game? Why would two teams go at each other verbally at a Church League Softball game? ("Now Ray, that is just a little too personal!") We are competitive people! And I can be personal, because it is personal to me. I am one of the most competitive people that I know. I hate to lose, especially in Church League Softball! But we need to take our competition to the enemy and not to our teammates. No team ever wins a championship when they do nothing but fight against their teammates. You only win when you come together for one common goal united against your opposition.

In the area of unity, the church could take a play from the playbook of sports.

Forty thousand fans were on hand in the Oakland stadium when Rickey Henderson tied Lou Brock's career stolen base record. According to USA Today Lou, who had left baseball in 1979, had followed Henderson's career and was excited about his success. Realizing that Rickey would set a new record, Brock said, "I'll be there. Do you think I'm going to miss it now? Rickey did in 12 years what took me 19. He's amazing." The real success stories in life are with

> *people who can rejoice in the successes of others. What Lou Brock did in cheering on Rickey Henderson should be a way of life in the family of God. Few circumstances give us a better opportunity to exhibit God's grace than when someone succeeds and surpasses us in an area of our own strength and reputation.*[5]

Why can't Christians celebrate when God works through other churches and other Christians? I mean, if athletes can do it for an individual trophy; at least we can unite our efforts around the trophy of grace!

Competition among churches and Christians runs just as deep, if not deeper, with so-called God-called ministers. Preachers make career moves in ministry rather than moving according to the Spirit of God. We have too many preachers who want to look good in their denomination rather than simply striving to please God. We have too many "Company" men and not enough "Kingdom" Men.

Jesus was un-competitively competitive. He knew that His fight was not against His own team, but against Satan and his army. In fact, He proves this in Scripture when attacked and accused of being a part of Satan's team.

> *23 So Jesus called them and spoke to them in parables: "How can Satan*

> *drive out Satan? 24 If a kingdom is divided against itself, that kingdom cannot stand. 25 If a house is divided against itself, that house cannot stand. 26 And if Satan opposes himself and is divided, he cannot stand; his end has come. 27 In fact, no one can enter a strong man's house and carry off his possessions unless he first ties up the strong man. Then he can rob his house.* (Mark 3:23-27)

It would serve well, if every Christian realized that a house divided against itself cannot stand. We are just fooling around and waiting for a great fall if we don't unite forces against Satan.

One leading factor of churches fighting against churches is because there are so many power hungry people in ministry today. Yet, Jesus was a "Kingdom Man", not a "Company Man". Everything Jesus did was credited back to His Heavenly Father. Note the following verses:

- *30 By myself I can do nothing; I judge only as I hear, and my judgment is just, for I seek not to please myself but him who sent me.* (John 5:30)
- *38 For I have come down from heaven not to do my will but to do the will of him who sent me.* (John 6:38)
- *16 Jesus answered, "My teaching is not my own.*

It comes from him who sent me." (John 7:16)

Jesus did not live His life so that He could receive credit for everything. He lived His life to give glory and honor back to His Heavenly Father. As Christians, so many times we get egos with church growth or jealous if another church outgrows the church where we worship. Our focus should rather be on Kingdom growth and giving glory to God with our lives!

We desperately need to make a comeback to following the example and calling of Jesus Christ to be Kingdom men and women.

> *January 3, 1993 will certainly be remembered in both Houston and Buffalo. Houston Oilers' and Buffalo Bills' fans watched with NFL viewers across the country as the Bills engineered the greatest comeback in NFL history. The Oilers led the football game at half-time 28-3. Quarterback Warren Moon had just completed the best half of his career. The half-time show included little else but talk of whom Houston would play next week as their last stop before the Super Bowl. Boomer Esiason warned his presumptuous co-commentators that Frank Reich was just the man to perform a miraculous comeback. Even*

Warren Moon used half time to warn his jubilant teammates that the game was far from over. But when Bubba McDowell opened the second half with a 58-yard touchdown interception that boosted the Oilers to a 35-3 lead, a comeback seemed virtually impossible. Everything changed in just 21 minutes. The fans at Rich Stadium in Orchard Park, New York saw the most unbelievable event unfold before their very eyes. The Bills overcame a 32-point deficit in the second-half and won the ballgame on a field goal in overtime. Football fans everywhere will never forget that game.[6]

In a world full of sin, suffering, and injustice, it seems sometimes as if God has been convincingly outscored by Satan. When such thoughts invade your mind, turn your attention to that football game. If such unlikely turn a rounds can transpire in the world of sports, then you can rest assured that God is gearing up for the most incredible comeback of all times.

(Well, I am about to preach, so turn the page only if you will open up your heart to God's Holy Word! And don't act surprised that I am going to preach! You didn't think a Baptist Preacher could write an entire book without preaching at least one sermon, did you?!)

A
Preaching
For
Priority
And
Perspective

"SINCE THE WAR IS ALREADY WON, WHY ARE WE LOSING THE BATTLE?!"
Luke 9:46-56

I think that the sermon title is a legitimate question! If Jesus already defeated Satan at the cross and empty tomb, why are Christians today seemingly losing the battle?

Gods' Word says in 2 Corinthians 11:14 that " . . . *Satan himself masquerades as an angel of light.*" The word "masquerade" is the Greek word "*meta-schematizo*" (met-askh-ay-mat-id'-zo); and means "to transfigure or disguise; figuratively, to apply (by accommodation)".[1] Satan disguises himself as one of us, and we cannot perceive whom we are really fighting against.

Growing up as a twin, my brother and I got into many fights. But fighting against Ricky, my twin brother, is kind of like hitting yourself! After you do it, you feel terrible, and the reality of it is - you both lost!! The same thing is happening in our churches today. Christians arguing against Christians, churches bitter against other churches. And who loses? God's Kingdom!

Satan has deceived so many people today. He has got so many of us fighting against ourselves, and we are losing the battle! Satan has always wanted to be like God, so he took a page out of God's playbook. In the Old Testament, several times God caused the enemy of the nation of Israel to kill and destroy its own nation. One example occurs in the life of Gideon.

19 Gideon and the hundred men with him reached the edge of the camp at the beginning of the middle watch, just after they had changed the guard. They blew their trumpets and broke the jars that were in their hands. 20 The three companies blew the trumpets and smashed the jars. Grasping the torches in their left hands and holding in their right hands the trumpets they were to blow, they shouted, "A sword for the LORD and for Gideon!" 21 While each man held his position around the camp, all the Midianites ran, crying out as they fled. 22 When the three hundred trumpets sounded, the LORD caused the men throughout the camp to turn on each other with their swords. (Judges 7:19-22)

Now Satan has in his arsenal the strategy and tactic to render Christians ineffective by tempting us to focus all our attention on fighting fellow Christians.

You see, this is manifested throughout our society today. Students shooting students, kids killing parents: this is just a physical manifestation of what so many churches are doing spiritually!

Look at what happens in Scripture, and we can get a glimpse of what Jesus wants us to know about really following Him.

46 An argument started among the disciples as to which of them would be the greatest. 47 Jesus, knowing their thoughts (Jesus knows our motives), *took a little child and had him stand beside him. 48 Then he said to them, "Whoever welcomes this little child in my name welcomes me; and whoever welcomes me welcomes the one who sent me. For he who is least among you all-he is the greatest." 49 "Master," said John, "we saw a man driving out demons in your name and we tried to stop him, because he is not one of us." 50 "Do not stop him," Jesus said, "for whoever is not against you is for you." 51 As the time approached for him to be taken up to heaven, Jesus resolutely set out for Jerusalem. 52 And he sent messengers on ahead, who went into a Samaritan village to get things ready for him; 53 but the people there did not welcome him, because he was heading for Jerusalem. 54 When the disciples James and John saw this, they asked, "Lord, do you want us to call fire down from heaven to destroy them? 55 But Jesus turned and rebuked them, 56 and they went to another village.* (Luke 9:46-56) [Parenthesis inserted by author]

Luke 9:46-56 reveals where the disciples were falling into the same trap that many church leaders are falling into today. Through God's Word, I want to show you a **Stark Reality**, and the **Sad Results**; but then I believe God would have us to know the **Saving Remedy**.

I. THE STARK REALITY – We are in the wrong fight! (46-50)

There are two reasons why we are in the wrong fight spiritually today.

A.) We have Misdirected our Focus. (46-48)

Jesus had this problem throughout his ministry with the disciples. The first time occurs, here in our text, about 6 months away from the cross when the disciples were with Jesus in Capernaum. (Mt. 18, Mark 9, and Luke 9) Perhaps this debate started with envy (three of the disciples had been with Jesus on the mount) or because of pride (the other nine had failed to cast out the demon). Also, just before this, Jesus had paid Peter's temple tax for him (Mt. 17); and this may have stirred up some envy. Jesus tells them that the first shall be last and the last shall be first. It happens again about three months away from the cross on the way to Jerusalem when the mother of James and John makes an unusual request of Jesus. (Mt. 20 and Mark 10). And Jesus told them, *"You don't know what you are asking. Can you drink the cup I drink and be baptized with the baptism that I am baptized with?"* As if it isn't bad enough that these two teachings didn't get through to the disciples; at the Last Supper, just a few days from the cross, a dispute arose among the disciples about who would be the greatest. (Luke 22). But Jesus will wash their feet as a demonstration of servanthood. And Jesus is teaching the spiritual truth of being little, being least, being less than the least in humility of spirit.

Preachers, church leaders, and church members are the same as the first disciples. Everybody always talks about three issues: Sunday School Averages, Square Footage or Acreage, and Size of the budget – the Almighty Dollar. If Christ sent today's churches a checklist of commendations and criticisms like those in Revelation 2-3, one of the things He would have "against" us would be staggering spiritual ambition. Our society thrives on ambition, and if we are not careful, we will bring our misdirected ambitions into the church.

OUR BIGGEST DETERRENT TO GREATNESS MAY BE THE DESIRE TO BE GREAT!

Our apparent zeal for God may only be an improper opposition toward our fellow man. Thus, we have misdirected our focus because of our own selfish ambitions and desires. Secondly, we are in the wrong fight because:

B. We have Mistaken our Foe (49-50)
In Luke 9, John didn't have a problem because he saw the man's results. John had a problem with the man, because he saw the man as a rival! John saw the man's casting out demons as competition to his ministry.

We are in the wrong fight – the bad fight. However, there are good fights out there. Three times in Scripture, Paul says that he fought the "good fight".

• 1 Timothy 1:18 *"Timothy, my son, I give you*

> *this instruction in keeping with the prophecies once made about you, so that by following them you may fight the good fight,"*
> - 1 Timothy 6:12 *"Fight the good fight of the faith. Take hold of the eternal life to which you were called when you made your good confession in the presence of many witnesses."*
> - 2 Timothy 4:7 *"I have fought the good fight, I have finished the race, I have kept the faith."*

There are fights we should be fighting. But, we are in a "bad fight". There is nothing wrong with fighting a good fight. That is what we ought to do. But we are fighting a bad fight, because we are fighting the wrong fight.

Scripture gives us an example of the fight we should be in.

> *11 Put on the full armor of God so that you can take your stand against the devil's schemes. 12 For our struggle is not against flesh and blood, but against the rulers, against the authorities, against the powers of this dark world and against the spiritual forces of evil in the heavenly realms.*
> (Ephesians 6:11-12)

Thus, the stark reality is that many Christians are in the wrong fight, because we have a misdirected focus and have mistaken our foe!

II. THE SAD RESULT – God's people lose sight! (51-56)

In our text from Luke 9, the disciples showed a lack of love for believers outside their own group. This is what we should expect from a "son of thunder". (Mark 3:17) Perhaps John was trying to impress Jesus with his zeal for protecting His Name, but the Lord was not impressed. Believers who think that their group is the only group God recognizes and blesses are in for a shock when they get to heaven.

We lose our focus on leading people to Christ. Christians start listing problems instead of leading people to the solution of the Saving Grace of Jesus Christ.

We shoot our own wounded, because we have gotten in the wrong battle. One example of this can be seen in the movie "Saving Private Ryan".

> *The first part of the movie is set during World War II during the invasion of Normandy at Omaha Beach. The American First Division would confront the best of the German coast divisions, the 352nd. D-Day - June 6, 1944. This pitted Hitler against Eisenhower. And for the Americans, everything went wrong. Only 2 of the 29 amphibious Sherman tanks with floatation screens made it to*

the beach. Throughout the landing, German gunners poured down deadly fire into the ranks of the invading Americans. They were in the wrong battle. They were in a battle they should have never been in and the casualties were great. The enemy deceived them and many Americans were shot and killed by their own men. They ended up winning the war, but they would lose too many in this battle. The Americans had lost 2400 men on that single day, June 6, 1944.[2]

The soldiers that lived that day learned a valuable lesson, and by the end of the day the Americans had landed 34,000 additional troops. We can learn a lot from D-Day for our spiritual journeys. And we could sure use the additional troops for God's Kingdom!

The Stark Reality is that many Christians are in the wrong fight. The Sad Results is that many of God's people lose sight of who the real enemy is and where the real battle ought to be fought. And God's Word gives us:

III. THE SAVING REMEDY – God's people must Unite!

God expresses the need for unity clearly in His Word.

1 As a prisoner for the Lord, then, I urge you to live a life worthy of the calling you have received. 2 Be completely humble and gentle; be patient, bearing with one another in love. 3 Make every effort to keep the unity of the Spirit through the bond of peace. 4 There is one body and one Spirit- just as you were called to one hope when you were called- 5 one Lord, one faith, one baptism; 6 one God and Father of all, who is over all and through all and in all." (Ephesians 4:1-6)

A. We need to Unite in our Target – Our target needs to be "whosoever" will call upon the name of the Lord. We specialize in everything today. We have doctors that specialize in one field, students who specialize in one major, stores that specialize in one product. While our world specializes in everything, God does not **S**pecialize, God **S**anctifies "whosoever" will! Maybe the following will give you some perspective:

- *It is one thing to be competitive in a **C**hurch Softball Game, It is another thing to be concerned with **C**alling people to **S**alvation.*
- *It is one thing to try to build the biggest church; it is another to answer God's call to Build the Kingdom.*
- *It is one thing to be competitive in Sunday*

School Attendance; it is another entirely differ-ent thing to be concerned with Heaven's Attendance!

- *It is one thing to have the biggest budget in your association; it is another thing entirely to invest in eternity!*
- *It is one thing to be asked to preach in the most revival services; it is totally different to be a servant in a worldwide revival!*

We desperately need to unite in our target of reaching lost people.

B. We need to Unite in our Tactic – to see the World come to know Jesus!
Jesus states His tactic in His Word.

20 My prayer is not for them alone. I pray also for those who will believe in me through their message, 21 that all of them may be one, Father, just as you are in me and I am in you. May they also be in us so that the world may believe that you have sent me. 22 I have given them the glory that you gave me, that they may be one as we are one: 23 I in them and you in me. May they be brought to complete unity to let the world know that you sent me and have loved them even as you have loved me. (John 17:20-23)

Before Jesus ascended to be with His Father in Heaven, He prayed for unity. Jesus knew that the success of the Christian ministry would be directly related to the unity of the Disciples of Christ.

> *One year, during my Seminary education, I found myself in Lake Yale, Florida for a Recreation Lab for Youth Ministers. While there, I had the opportunity to travel to a prison in Cocoa Beach, Florida with a sports evangelism team. While we were playing the prisoners in basketball and softball, I recognized that there were several hundred inmates in the prison yard, but only a handful of prison guards. And to top that off, the guards had no weapons other than a nightstick through a loop on their belts. Observing this, I approached one guard with, what I thought was, a good question. I asked him, "Aren't you scared that these prisoners are going to gang up on you and attack you to gain their freedom from their prison?" And I will never forget the guard's response. He just looked at me, smiled, and said, "Lunatics never Unite!" Lunatics never unite. And that*

is when it pierced my heart. We Christians would be sheer lunatics to keep fighting against ourselves and not unite for the cause of Christ and His Kingdom!!! So let us all stop fooling around and start following Jesus – Together!!

CHAPTER 8

"Arrogantly Humble"

CHAPTER TRUTH:

Christians boast about being humble yet seldom boast in the Lord!

Did you hear about the minister who said he had a wonderful sermon on humility but was waiting for a large crowd before preaching it?[1] Doesn't make a lot of sense does it? I mean, when people tell you that they are humble, that sort of defeats the purpose, doesn't it? M.R. De Haan used to say, *"Humility is something we should constantly pray for, yet never thank God that we have."* [2]

My father used to say things like, "Son, your head is getting too big for your shoulders." Or my Dad would say, "You are getting a little too big for your pants." Now, I know what my Dad meant. What he meant was, "I was getting a little too cocky for my own good." And when Christians are prideful, they are no good for the Kingdom. My earthly Dad could discern when I had an air about my spirit that didn't need to exist. My Heavenly Father knows even better the motivations of my heart.

It is possible in the Christian life to do all the right things for all the wrong reasons. You can preach, teach, and disciple people, because you have an inward craving to be viewed as influential by your peers. If you are fooling around in your spiritual journey, it is easy to get an ego boost through ministry. But when you are truly following Christ, you recognize that you can influence people for a moment, while God can impact people for a lifetime!

Serving as a Pastor is a truly humbling experience. First of all, realizing that God allows me to preach His Word and called me into His ministry is a humbling encounter. But church members have a way of keeping the minister in his proper place. One Sunday after a sermon, a lady approached me at the back of the sanctuary and said, "Every sermon you preach gets better than the next." Talk about humbling! I think I know what she meant to express, but what came across to me was that the first sermon I preached was the best I was ever going to do. The rest of the sermons are going to be all down hill from there! There is really no room for egos and prideful spirits in the ministry of the Lord.

Just listen to a small list of Scripture on humility.

- *"The LORD sustains the humble but casts the wicked to the ground."* (Psalm 147:6)
- *"For the LORD takes delight in his people; he crowns the humble with salvation."* (Psalm 149:4)
- *"He mocks proud mockers but gives grace to the humble."* (Proverbs 3:34)

- *"Humble yourselves before the Lord, and he will lift you up."* (James 4:10)
- *"Humble yourselves, therefore, under God's mighty hand, that he may lift you up in due time."* (1 Peter 5:6-7)

God spoke often in His Word about humility. It was Pride that caused Satan's fall to begin with. He always wanted to be like God. So Satan does not want to go down alone. The same thing that led to his downfall seems to be the devil's number one temptation to those serving God. Satan desires to tempt the believer into the mindset that, "I am smart enough to make it on my own, and I don't really need God in my life." This is explained through a story about the great preacher Dr. Harry Ironside.

> *Dr. Harry Ironside was once convicted about his lack of humility. A friend recommended as a remedy, that he march through the streets of Chicago wearing a sandwich board, shouting the scripture verses on the board for all to hear. Dr. Ironside agreed to this venture and when he returned to his study and removed the board, he said, "I'll bet there's not another man in town who would do that."* [3]

If you fool around in your spiritual walk, Satan will

deceive you into thinking more highly of yourselves than you ought.

It was the great D.L. Moody who said, *"Be humble or you will stumble."* [4] And stumble many have. Many have focused on themselves rather than on their Savior and have traded following Jesus for following their desires. The following story of two ships represents many spiritual lives that have been lost at the seas of selfishness and self-centeredness.

> *In the summer of 1986, two ships collided in the Black Sea off the coast of Russia. Hundreds of passengers died as they were hurled into the icy waters below. News of the disaster was further darkened when an investigation revealed the cause of the accident. It wasn't a technology problem like radar malfunction—or even thick fog. The cause was human stubbornness. Each captain was aware of the other ship's presence nearby. Both could have steered clear, but according to news reports, neither captain wanted to give way to the other. Each was too proud to yield first. By the time they came to their senses, it was too late.* [5]

By not yielding to Christ, many have gone on an ego

trip that they have yet to recover from.

How do you follow Jesus and not fool around when it comes to humility? If I told you how I stay humble, I wouldn't be too humble, would I? (And since I have just as bad of a problem with humility as you, the reader does, I will try a different approach.) Maybe we can learn from some of the humble men throughout history.

- *Hudson Taylor was scheduled to speak at a Large Presbyterian church in Melbourne, Australia. The moderator of the service introduced the missionary in eloquent and glowing terms. He told the large congregation all that Taylor had accomplished in China, and then presented him as "our illustrious guest". Taylor stood quietly for a moment, and then opened his message by saying, "Dear friends, I am the little servant of an illustrious Master."* [6]

- *Wakefield tells the story of the famous inventor Samuel Morse who was once asked if he ever encountered situations where he didn't know what to do. Morse responded, "More than once, and whenever I could not see my way clearly, I knelt down and prayed to God for light and understanding." Morse received many honors from his invention of the telegraph but felt undeserving: "I have made a valuable application of electricity not because I was superior to other men but solely because God, who meant it for mankind, must reveal it to someone and He was pleased to reveal it to me."* [7]

- *Winston Churchill was once asked, "Doesn't it thrill you to know that every time you make a speech, the hall is packed to overflowing?" "It's quite flattering," replied Sir Winston. "But whenever I feel that way, I always remember that if instead of making a political speech I was being hanged, the crowd would be twice as big."* [8]

- *It was John Riskin who said, "I believe the first test of a truly great man is his humility. I do not mean by humility, doubt of his own power, or hesitation in speaking his opinion. But really great men have a ... feeling that the greatness is not in them but through them; that they could not do or be anything else than God made them."* [9]

- *Andrew Murray said, "The humble man feels no jealousy or envy. He can praise God when others are preferred and blessed before him. He can bear to hear others praised while he is forgotten because ... he has received the spirit of Jesus, who pleased not Himself, and who sought not His own honor. Therefore, in putting on the Lord Jesus Christ he has put on the heart of compassion, kindness, meekness, longsuffering, and humility."* [10]

- *It is possible to be too big for God to use you but never too small for God to use you.* [11]

- *"They that know God will be humble," John Flavel has said, " and they that know themselves cannot be proud."* [12]

- *Phillip Brooks made an apt comment when he said, "The true way to be humble is not to stoop until you are smaller than yourself, but to stand at your real height against some higher nature that will show you what the real smallness of your greatness is."* [13]

Do you see the common thread that runs through humble mankind? In every story or quote, humble men recognize that only God can create greatness, because only God is great! When you recognize that He alone is worthy, you pale in comparison to what little you have to offer.

I love the following story related to humility.

> *On a visit to the Beethoven museum in Bonn, a young American student became fascinated by the piano on which Beethoven had composed some of his greatest works. She asked the museum guard if she could play a few bars on it; she accompanied the request with a lavish tip, and the guard agreed.*

The girl went to the piano and tinkled out the opening of the Moonlight Sonata. As she was leaving she said to the guard, "I suppose all the great pianist who come here want to play on that piano."

The guard shook his head. "Padarewski [the famed Polish pianist] was here a few years ago and he said he wasn't worthy to touch it." [14]

We are not worthy to even touch or see the holiness of a Righteous God. When we realize how awesome and holy God is, you humbly realize how pitiful and sinful you are!

When you are tempted to boast about your humility, remember what the Living Word says.

26 Brothers, think of what you were when you were called. Not many of you were wise by human standards; not many were influential; not many were of noble birth. 27 But God chose the foolish things of the world to shame the wise; God chose the weak things of the world to shame the strong. 28 He chose the lowly things of this world and the despised things-and the things that are not-to nullify the things that are, 29 so that no one may

> *boast before him. 30 It is because of*
> *him that you are in Christ Jesus, who*
> *has become for us wisdom from God-*
> *that is, our righteousness, holiness*
> *and redemption. 31 Therefore, as it is*
> *written: "Let him who boasts boast in*
> *the Lord."*
> (1 Corinthians 1:26-31)

If we are going to boast in something, at least we can boast in something that will never fail us – the Lord Almighty. Remember when you were little, and you would boast about what your daddy could do or even in what you could do? But the truth would always come out, and it was discovered that your daddy was not an astronaut on the last space shuttle, and you could not bench press 225 lbs in the 4th grade. The truth will always come out! So why not boast in The One who can always back up what you are boasting about. If you boast in the Lord, He will always back it up! Always has – always will!!

While many of us are arrogantly humble, I am so glad that Jesus Christ has the attitude of humility. No biblical text resembles the humility of Jesus like Philippians 2:8.

> *8 And being found in appearance as a*
> *man, he humbled himself and became*
> *obedient to death- even death on a*
> *cross!*

What an incredible display of humbleness. The Living Lord, Sovereign Savior, Prince of Peace, and Creator of creation humbled Himself and took on our sin so that we might have life abundantly. Jesus didn't talk about humility; Christ displayed it between two thieves and a jeering crowd. Jesus is the author and perfector of our faith and the Master model for humility!

One more thing while we are on this concept of humility; living a humble life is a great way to witness to a lost world about Christ. One more story for example: (Sorry about all the illustrations in this chapter. But I would not be truthfully revealing how to be humble if all I gave were illustrations of how humble I was. That would be another oxymoron, and I would be a spiritual moron if I did!)

Many years ago, Christian professor Stuart Blackie of the University of Edinburgh was listening to his students as they presented oral readings. When one young man rose to begin his recitation, he held his book in the wrong hand. The professor thundered, "Take your book in your right hand, and be seated!" At this harsh rebuke, the student held up his right arm. He didn't have a right hand! The other students shifted uneasily in their chairs. For a moment the professor hesitated. Then he made his way to the student, put his arm around him, and with tears streaming from his eyes, said, "I never knew about it. Please, will you forgive me?" His humble apology made a lasting impact on that young man. This story was told some time later in a large gathering of believers. At the close of the meeting a man came forward, turned to the crowd, and raised his right arm. It ended at the wrist. He said, "I was that student. Professor Blackie led me to Christ. But he never could have done it if he had not made the wrong right." [15]

The more you fool around, the more highly you think of yourself. The more you follow Jesus, the more you realize how hopeless and helpless you are without Him. And when you follow in His greatness, people start to see the magnitude of Christ shining a message through your yielded and God-dependant life! (And that will cause you to boast in the awesome grace and love of a Savior that not only saves you, but also chooses to manifest His life through you!)

CHAPTER 9

"Servant Masters"

CHAPTER TRUTH:

We wish for people to sacrificially serve God, but we will only serve God until we have to make a sacrifice!

When it comes to being a servant for our Savior, most Christians can talk the talk but fall miserably when it comes to their walk. The church has allowed the pull of the world towards being your own boss to push within the Christian realm. We are allowing selfish attitudes towards worship styles, times or days of worship services, and even the colors of the carpet to split churches down the middle. This would not happen in churches if people were willing to consider others as more important than themselves. I mean, when is the last time that you heard that a church split over doctrine. Most churches divide because people cannot serve each other with the same attitude as that of Christ.

Maybe most Christians are having a hard time becoming servants because most of their church leadership struggles in the same area. It is not hard at all to find a pastor who preaches on service, but would rather be served. For example, in the middle of a sermon series on "Being a Christian Servant", a pastor might get upset during a business meeting because he didn't get what he wanted. We will preach on serving others and then conduct business meetings like "You are wrong if you don't agree with me." We say, "Serving God means being able to agree to disagree", yet pastors sometimes pick up and leave the first time a church vote doesn't go their way.

True servanthood has regressed to such a state in our world today that most people don't even like to be referred to as a servant. Even people that get paid to be servants would rather go by a different title. For instance, waiters are servants, but nobody calls them by their real job. (I have always wondered why they are called waiters, because the customer is the one who is always waiting!) Well, anyway, in our society, it is not the popular thing to serve other people. The motto in our society is move to the top of the ladder and step on anyone you have to in order to get there.

This is not a new problem with our generation. The disciples of Jesus had the same problem in the first century that we struggle with in the 21st century. As was mentioned in the section "A Preaching for Priority and Perspective", Jesus' disciples argued about who was going to be the greatest while they were supposedly leaving it all to follow Jesus.

> *46 An argument started among the disciples as to which of them would be*

the greatest. 47 Jesus, knowing their thoughts, took a little child and had him stand beside him. 48 Then he said to them, "Whoever welcomes this little child in my name welcomes me; and whoever welcomes me welcomes the one who sent me. For he who is least among you all-he is the greatest."
(Luke 9:46-48)

So the disciples are arguing about where they are going to sit rather than dropping to their knees and serving the lost world around them.

But Christians today are no different. We all have the common struggle of knowing we are suppose to serve while at the same time having our fleshly nature screaming for power and prestige. That's why Jesus taught often on the subject of servanthood while He was with His disciples. Just notice a few of Jesus' words to His followers.

- *"A student is not above his teacher, nor a servant above his master. It is enough for the student to be like his teacher, and the servant like his master."* (Matthew 10:24)

- *"The greatest among you will be your servant. For whoever exalts himself will be humbled, and whoever humbles himself will be exalted."* (Matthew 23:11-12)

- *"Sitting down, Jesus called the Twelve and said, 'If anyone wants to be first, he must be the very last, and the servant of all.'"* (Mark 9:35)

- *"No servant can serve two masters. Either he will hate the one and love the other, or he will be devoted to the one and despise the other. You cannot serve both God and Money."* (Luke 16:13)

- *"Remember the words I spoke to you: 'No servant is greater than his master.'"* (John 15:20)

Jesus sure did have a lot to say about being a servant! Jesus promises to exalt those who humble themselves and to place first, one day, those who today are willing to be last. In fact, look at Jesus' final words in the parable of the talents. (I know you probably have seen it before, but this time look very closely and try to see it with the eyes of your heart.)

> *21 His master replied, "Well done, good and faithful **servant**! You have been faithful with a few things; I will put you in charge of many things. Come and share your master's happiness!" 22 The man with the two talents also came. "Master," he said, "you entrusted me with two talents; see, I have gained two more." 23 His master replied, "Well done, good and faithful **servant**! You*

*have been faithful with a few things; I
will put you in charge of many things.
Come and share your master's happi-
ness!"*
(Matthew 25:21-23) [Emphasis added
by author]

Did you see it? I mean, really see it? "Well done, good
and faithful SERVANT." Now, I don't know of one
Christian that does not want to hear Jesus make that
same statement to him or her one-day. But in order for
Jesus to say, "Well done, good and faithful servant!";
you would have to have been a servant. Jesus will never
lie to make you feel good. The Truth that sets you free
will never exaggerate and give you a title that is not
reflective of your life. Therefore, in order to be
rewarded as a servant one day, you better start becoming a servant today!

Further study on servanthood in God's Word may
encourage you to be a servant rather than just say you
are one. "Servant" in our New Testament usually represents the Greek word *doulos*, which means, "bond-
slave". Sometimes the New Testament word is
diakonos, which translates as "deacon or minister".
These two Greek words *doulos* and *diakonos* are
synonyms.[1] Both words denote a man who is not at his
own disposal, but is his master's purchased property. A
servant is bought to serve his master's needs, to be at
his beck and call. The slave's sole business is to do as
he is told. Christian service therefore means, first and

foremost, living out a slave relationship to one's Savior (1 Corinthians 6:19-20).

The following discussion on servanthood provides deeper understanding.

> *The way that they serve him, he tells them, is by becoming the slaves of their fellow-servants and being willing to do literally anything, however costly, irksome, or undignified, in order to help them. This is what the Lord means, as he himself showed at the Last supper when he played the slave's part and washed the disciples' feet.* [2]

James Packer goes on to discuss how it is possible for humans with a selfish nature to serve the Master of their lives.

> *Only the Holy Spirit can create in us the kind of love toward our Savior that will overflow in imaginative sympathy and practical helpfulness towards his people. Unless the spirit is training us in love, we are not fit persons to go to college or a training class to learn the know-how or particular branches of Christian work. Gifted leaders who are self-centered and loveless are a blight to the church rather than a blessing.* [3]

Boy, do we ever need more practicing Christian servants. The Lord knows that we have enough professing ones!

In a world full of professing servants that really want to be their own boss, I'm so glad that Jesus was The Master who was also a real servant! In fact, Jesus was the MASTER SERVANT! He was the best of the best at becoming the least of the least. He was on top at allowing Himself to be placed at the bottom. In Jesus, we have the Creator dying for His Creation. In Christ, we have one who knew no sin willing to become sin on our behalf. Scripture is replete with pictures of our MASTER SERVANT. There is no greater servant verse in all of the Old Testament than the suffering servant passage.

> *Who has believed our message and to whom has the arm of the LORD been revealed? 2 He grew up before him like a tender shoot, and like a root out of dry ground. He had no beauty or majesty to attract us to him, nothing in his appearance that we should desire him. 3 He was despised and rejected by men, a man of sorrows, and familiar with suffering. Like one from whom men hide their faces he was despised, and we esteemed him not. 4 Surely he took up our infirmities and carried our sorrows, yet we considered him stricken by God, smitten by him, and afflicted. 5 But he*

was pierced for our transgressions, he was crushed for our iniquities; the punishment that brought us peace was upon him, and by his wounds we are healed. 6 We all, like sheep, have gone astray, each of us has turned to his own way; and the LORD has laid on him the iniquity of us all. 7 He was oppressed and afflicted, yet he did not open his mouth; he was led like a lamb to the slaughter, and as a sheep before her shearers is silent, so he did not open his mouth. 8 By oppression and judgment he was taken away. And who can speak of his descendants? For he was cut off from the land of the living; for the transgression of my people he was stricken. 9 He was assigned a grave with the wicked, and with the rich in his death, though he had done no violence, nor was any deceit in his mouth. 10 Yet it was the LORD's will to crush him and cause him to suffer, and though the LORD makes his life a guilt offering, he will see his offspring and prolong his days, and the will of the LORD will prosper in his hand. 11 After the suffering of his soul, he will see the light [of life] and be satisfied; by his knowledge my righteous servant will justify

*many, and he will bear their iniqui-
ties. 12 Therefore I will give him a
portion among the great, and he will
divide the spoils with the strong,
because he poured out his life unto
death, and was numbered with the
transgressors. For he bore the sin of
many, and made intercession for the
transgressors.* (Isaiah 53:1-12)

And a profound New Testament servant text is:

*"For even the Son of Man did not
come to be served, but to serve, and to
give his life as a ransom for many."*
(Mark 10:45)

What a great purpose statement! What a grand role model for all of us to follow!! If Christians would really start modeling the servanthood of their Master instead of being their own boss (a.k.a – fooling around); then they would be much closer to truly following Jesus!

Maybe the main reason we Christians have such a tough time being servants is that we like being in prominent positions. We strive to become smarter, stronger, richer, and wiser. The world around us tells us that you have to be big to become somebody. This country screams that in order to call the shots, you have to be a big shot. Maybe we are too big for All-powerful Jesus to work through us! Or perhaps we are so prone to be our own boss, that God chooses not to play second in line to our own wishes and desires. If we would ever realize how small we are in comparison to the vastness and incomprehendable greatness of our God, we would want more than anything for Him to call the shots in our lives. It is only when we serve the master that we get what we could never amass on our own power. And that is the all-powerful God of this universe working through small, dependable, worthless individuals like myself. One powerful story to prove the point that God can do a lot with a little:

In 1972, NASA launched the exploratory space probe Pioneer 10. According to Leon Jaroff in Time, the satellite's primary mission was to reach Jupiter, photograph the planet and its moons, and beam data to earth about Jupiter's magnetic field, radiation belts, and atmosphere. Scientists regarded this as a bold plan, for at that time no earth satellite had ever gone beyond Mars, and they feared the asteroid belt would destroy the satellite before it could reach its target. But Pioneer 10 accomplished its mission and much, much more. Swinging past the giant planet in November 1973, Jupiter's immense gravity hurled Pioneer 10 at a higher rate of speed toward the edge of the solar system. At one billion miles from the sun, Pioneer 10 passed Saturn. At some two billion miles, it hurtled past Uranus; Neptune at nearly three billion miles; Pluto at almost four billion miles. By 1997, twenty-five years after its launch, Pioneer 10 was more than six billion miles from the sun.

And despite that immense distance, Pioneer 10 continued to beam back radio signals to scientists on Earth. "Perhaps most remarkable," writes Jaroff, "those signals emanate from an 8-watt transmitter, which radiates about as much power as a bedroom night light, and takes more than nine hours to reach Earth.'" The Little Satellite That Could was not qualified to do what it did. Engineers designed Pioneer 10 with a useful life of just three years. But it kept going and going. By simple longevity, its tiny 8-watt transmitter radio accomplished more than anyone thought possible.

So it is when we offer ourselves to serve the Lord. God can work even through someone with 8-watt abilities.[4]

If we are willing to swallow our pride and serve Christ, He can do with our lives more than we ever thought was possible!

A Final Pause With A Purpose

C arter, my son, is almost 2 years old. His most often utilized word is the two-letter word "No." He says it at least 200 times a day.

> *"Carter, do you want something to eat?" "No."*
> *"Carter, do you want a spat?" "No."*
> *"Carter, do you love daddy?" "No."*
> *"Carter, do you want to go play?" "Carter, play." (Still no "yes.")*

I know that as Carter continues to grow, one day soon he will learn to say "yes." But for now, Carter loves to play around and has an awfully hard time saying, "yes" to the things of life. Isn't Carter just like all of us students and adults? For most of us Christians, it is easier to play around than admit, "Yes, we need to start following Jesus." But we all have to grow up one day and be willing to admit that "Yes, we are a long way from becoming what God desires for us to be." Maybe throughout this book, you have grown up enough to admit that, "Yes, sometimes I am genuinely hypocritical rather than being truly real." Or "Yes, I have been inconsistent in my walk with the never changing Christ." And, "Yes, I crave God's forgiveness, and I have a difficult time forgiving others around me." Hopefully, as you do more following Jesus and less fooling around, it will be easier for you to admit your weaknesses in your walk with Christ.

As Amanda and Carter are fast asleep in the master bedroom, I sit in the darkness of the living room, except for the little light emanating from my laptop computer. It is just past midnight on a Friday night. As I sit in the darkness, I realize that most of my spiritual life is darker than God desires for it to be. And I must admit, that far too often, I have been fast asleep in the presence of my Master, when I should have been following closely in His steps. The author of this book has discovered throughout this writing that he desperately needs to be in touch with the Author of life more regularly. I also must admit that "Yes," – there I said it; "Yes, I need to stop fooling around with the life God has blessed me with and follow Christ each and every waking moment of my life!"

So this pause is for a purpose. Admittance (Saying "Yes") is the hardest, but most essential and primary step in salvation. Daily admittance is also the most precious step in the application of God's truth in your everyday life. Most preachers do a good job of telling (shouting out) what you need to do. However, most never get around to telling you how to do what you need to do. Therefore, this last chapter is the "How-to-do-it" chapter! This next chapter is the application of the truth found in the previous 9 chapters. Hopefully, the Holy Spirit has lovingly convicted you throughout this book of your tendency to fool around more than you follow Christ. Maybe some of those oxymorons hit too close to home and described how at times you and I have played the fool, spiritually. Well, God's Word has a wake-up call for all of us to come out of the darkness and live in the blessed light! So only after you are willing to say, "Yes." – ("Yes, I am not where I need to be in my walk with Christ"); turn the page and see "How to Start Following Jesus and Stop Fooling Around!"

CHAPTER 10

"How to Follow Jesus And Stop Fooling Around!"

CHAPTER TRUTH:

If you are truly following Jesus, you won't have time to fool around!

Perhaps you have heard of the three churches at the intersection of Broadway and Main streets. One Sunday evening, the congregation in one church was singing, "Will there be any stars in my crown?" while just across the street they were intoning, "No, not one, no, not one." At the same time the church on the third corner was chanting, "Oh, that will be glory for me, glory for me." [1]

Maybe we wouldn't fool around as much if we all concentrated on our own spiritual lives. At the beginning of this chapter of application, I want to warn you not to read this chapter in order to solve somebody else's spiritual problem. As you read this chapter, open up your heart and let God deal with you personally.

A news item from Los Angeles shows that Judge Yankwich had such a case as to make judges want to scream.

Luther Wright and Hermann Rongg appeared before Federal Judge Leon R. Yankwich, each claiming ownership of a patent. The judge attempted to moderate the dispute, declaring:

"Well, one of you must be wrong."

"That's right," declared Rongg. "I'm Rongg, and I'm right."

Then Wright interrupted: "He's wrong, your honor. I'm right and Rongg is wrong."

But largely upon the strength of a letter Wright wrote Rongg, Judge Yankwich ruled the Wright-Rongg dispute as follows:

"Paradoxical though it may appear in this case, Wright is wrong and Rongg is right, and I so enter judgment." [2]

This chapter is not for you to determine who is wrong and who is right. As you can see from the previous story, sometimes that can be very difficult! Rather than focusing on your past failures or successes, discover how you can stop fooling around and start following Jesus today!

Look with me at Luke, chapter 9, beginning with

the 23rd verse.

I want you to see verse 23, first in the Living Bible paraphrase.

> *Then he said to all, "Anyone who wants to follow me must put aside his own desires and conveniences and carry his cross with him every day and keep close to me!"* **Luke 9:23 (TLB)**

So, this passage of Scripture is for those who wish to follow Jesus. Let's look at the passage in its entirety from the New International Version.

> *23 Then he said to them all: "If anyone would come after me, he must deny himself and take up his cross daily and follow me. 24 For whoever wants to save his life will lose it, but whoever loses his life for me will save it. 25 What good is it for a man to gain the whole world, and yet lose or forfeit his very self? 26 If anyone is ashamed of me and my words, the Son of Man will be ashamed of him when he comes in his glory and in the glory of the Father and of the holy angels. 27 I tell you the truth, some who are standing here will not taste death before they see the kingdom of God." Luke 9:23-27*

How do you follow Jesus and stop fooling around?

First, You must have a <u>desire</u> to follow Jesus? (vs. 23)

*"If anyone **will come** after me . . ."* (NIV)

*"Anyone **who wants to follow** me . . ."* (TLB)

*"If anyone **wishes to come after Me** . . ."* (NASU)

*"If any of you **wants to be my follower** . . ."* (NLT)

"If anyone wishes, desires, longs to, really wants to come after me..." Do you have a passion for Jesus Christ because he loved you enough to send his Son to die for you? *"For God so loved the world that He **gave** ..."* (John 3:16) 1 John 4:19 says, *"We love because He first loved us."* Therefore, if we fail to love Christ with all our heart, soul, mind, and strength; are we telling Jesus that His love and sacrifice were not enough for us to love him with our all in return?! What more could Christ have done to make you love him any more? Then why don't we? You have to want Jesus more than anything in life! What could be more important?

When asked to follow Jesus, some replied, "WAIT let me first go bury my dead." It was not that Jesus did not want them to love their own kin, but to love Him more than anything. The reason we don't have more people witnessing in the church is not because of fear, but due to lack of concern. Do you really desire to follow Jesus? You must! Desire is the first step towards truly following Jesus. You have to want to bad enough to do it!

Have you come to the place in your life that you want to follow Jesus more than you desire to fool around?

Second, You must <u>Deny</u> Yourself. (vs. 23, 24-25)

*" . . . he must **deny himself** . . ."* (NIV)

*" . . . must **put aside his own desires and conveniences** . . ."* (TLB)

*" . . . you must **put aside your selfish ambition,** . . ."* (NLT)

> *"For whoever wants to save his life will lose it, but whoever loses his life for me will save it." What good is it for a man to gain the whole world, and yet lose or forfeit his very self?* (vs. 24-25)

Only when we place Christ above all, can we deny ourselves. Pride has kept more people from an intimate relationship with Jesus than any other thing. Sometimes we think of ourselves more highly than we really are. Only when we stand against the Cross, that *"Great*

Leveler of Men" [3] as A. T. Robertson called it, can we not think more highly of ourselves than we ought. Christ himself must be our standard.

Jim Calvert responded to an inner tug in his heart to serve as a missionary to a fierce tribe in the Fiji Islands. As the ship reached the islands, the captain warned Calvert that he would surely die in the effort. Calvert replied, *"I died before I got here."* [4] Only those who give up their lives find them!!

During his reign, King Frederick William III of Prussia found himself in trouble. Wars had been costly, and in trying to build the nation, he was seriously short of finances. He couldn't disappoint his people and to give in to the enemy was unthinkable. After careful reflection, he decided to ask the women of Prussia to bring their gold and silver jewelry to be melted down for their country. For each ornament received, he determined to exchange a decoration of bronze or iron as a symbol of his gratitude. Each decoration would be inscribed, "I gave gold for iron, 1813." The response was overwhelming. Even more importantly, these women prized their gifts from the king more highly than their former jewelry. The reason, of course, was clear. The decorations were proof that they had sacrificed for their king. Indeed, it became unfashionable to wear jewelry, and thus was established the Order of the Iron Cross. Members wore no ornaments except a cross of iron for all to see.[5]

When Christians come to their King, they too,

exchange the flourishes of their former life for a cross. And they come to cherish the cross more! To follow Jesus, you must deny yourself!

Third, You must Take Up His Cross <u>Daily</u>. (vs. 23, 26)

*". . . and **take up his cross daily**. . ."* (NIV)

*" . . . and **carry his cross with him every day** . . ."* (TLB)

*" . . . **shoulder your cross daily**, . . ."* (NLT)

> *"If anyone is ashamed of me and my words, the Son of Man will be ashamed of him when he comes in his glory and in the glory of the Father and of the holy angels."* (vs. 26)

If you are ashamed of Jesus, you can't take up your cross daily. *"I am not ashamed of the gospel, because it is the power of God for the salvation of everyone who believes . . ."* (Romans 1:16)

But what does it mean to carry the cross? What did carrying the cross cost Jesus?" It cost Him persecution, His pride, His life. It brought personal eternity to all who would accept his sacrificial death and glorious resurrection. And carrying the cross of Jesus brings peace to one's life.

Spurgeon said, *"There are no crown- wearers in heaven that were not cross- bearers here below."* [6]

Please read carefully the following illustration entitled, *"God does count crosses."*

> *"I counted dollars while God counted crosses,*
> *I counted gains while He counted losses.*
> *I counted by worth by the things gained in store,*
> *but He sized me up by the scars that I bore.*
> *I coveted honors and sought for degrees,*
> *He wept as He counted the hours on my knees.*
> *I never knew until one day by the grave,*
> *how vain are the things that we spend life to save."* [7]

God counts the crosses that we carry for Him. If we are ashamed of Him here on earth, He will be ashamed of us one day to come. Because of Jesus, the crosses we carry have the power to save the lives of the lost around us.

> *On Feb. 3, 1943, the troop ship Dorchester went down in the icy Atlantic*

off the tip of Greenland with heavy loss of life. It was not the worst disaster of a long war, but we have good reason to remember it. There were four chaplains aboard who were dedicated to carrying the cross of Jesus. George L. Fox and Clark V. Poling were Protestant ministers, Alexander D. Goode was a Jewish Rabbi, and John P. Washington was a Catholic priest. When the torpedoes struck around 1:00 A.M., many of the inexperienced GI's were caught sleeping without their lifejackets, although that was contrary to orders. In the fight to survive, many were left without them. Each of the four chaplains wore lifejackets when they were helping the wounded, calming the shocked, etc. The chaplains declined places in the emergency rafts. When last seen in the light of the flares, just before the ship went down, not one of the chaplains wore a lifejacket. Their lifejacket's had been forced on unwilling soldiers taught to obey the order of their superiors. These four dedicated men stood together arm-in-arm praying for those young men of America for whom now only prayers were left. [8]

You see, we must carry our crosses in a world lacking spiritual lifejackets – (The Savior). We must start following Jesus and quit fooling around.

Therefore, in order for us to follow Jesus, we must desire to, deny ourselves, and daily take up our cross. When we follow those three steps outlined by our Savior in Luke 9:23, then look at the results.

The Results

" *. . . and Follow Me.*" (NIV)

" *. . . and keep close to me! . . .*" (TLB)

This is what it means to follow Jesus. This theme of denying yourself, taking up your cross daily, and following Jesus is seen throughout the Scripture. It should be the purpose of our lives because it was the purpose of Jesus' life.

John 20:21 Jesus says, "As the Father sent Me, so I am sending you." How did the Father send Jesus? What was His purpose in life? Each one of the gospel writers, inspired by the Holy Spirit, gives us a reason why Jesus came.

A.) Matthew 20:28 and Mark 10:45 both give us the same reason Jesus came.

"Jesus did not come to be served, but to serve."

If, as the Father sent Jesus, so He sends us; we must live not to be served, but to serve. Dr. Rick Warren says that the mark of spiritual maturity occurs when a believer, *"takes off the bib and puts on an apron"*.[9] Immature children wear bibs and expect others to meet their needs. Those who don aprons have learned the joy of serving others. If Jesus came to serve, we must also. Now look back at Luke 9:23 - *"Deny Yourself"*. In order to serve, we must do what it takes to follow Jesus - deny ourselves.

B.) Luke 19:10 gives us another reason why Jesus came.

"I have come to seek and save the lost".

As Jesus came, so He sends us. Through the power of the Holy Spirit, we come to seek and save the lost. Now look back at Luke 9:23 - *"Take Up His Cross"*. The Cross of Jesus is the only thing that can save a lost and dying world!

C.) John 10:10 gives us the third reason why Jesus came.

"I have come that they might have life and that they might have it more abundantly."

John 10:4 states, *"His Sheep follow Him because they know His voice."* Following Jesus is the only way to an abundant life! Do you know His Voice? If so, follow Him and stop fooling around.

Luke 9:23 says, *"Follow Me"*. We must do just that to experience the abundant life! Remember that you are not fooling anybody but yourself and a lost and dying world that needs Jesus. They need to see the cross that you carry!

In conclusion, please note the following story.

> *Football's "Wrongest Run" occurred in the 1929 Rose Bowl. California was leading Georgia Tech 7-6, when California's Roy Riegels picked up the football and began running the wrong direction. He became confused when California players began blocking Tech men behind him. He turned and ran in that direction. The crowd roared in amazement, "Wrong Way! Wrong Way!" Benny Lom, a fast California halfback, started after Riegels, who was headed straight for the opponent's goal line. "Roy, Roy, stop!" he cried. But the noise was so great that Riegels thought that the crowd was cheering him on. Just as he reached the goal line, his teammate tackled him. After the mishap, the California team tried to punt from their one-yard line. But Georgia Tech blocked the punt and fell on the ball in the end zone for a two- point safety. This proved to be Georgia Tech's margin of victory!* [10]

Are we running the wrong way in our Christian lives?

Better yet, are you running the "wrongest run" when you compare your actions to the character of Christ? Another necessary but tough question: Are the Christians that are fooling around giving Satan enough margin for victory over our lives and the lives of those who need salvation. (Now, I know that God has already won the final victory, but why then, are Christians losing so many of the battles?!)

Ok, I promise, - last illustration. (Remember I am a Baptist Preacher!)

> *Two Christians were driving through an area where the road was being widened. At the end of the repair zone, a sign informed travelers, "Construction Ended. Thank You for Your Patience."* [11]

One day, we will arrive in heaven to enter the presence of Jesus, and we will see Him face to face. Until then, our spiritual lives are in constant "construction" stage. I don't know about you, but when I arrive in heaven, I am going to thank my Savior for His Perfect Patience. I think I will even do it right now!

> *Lord Jesus, thank You so much for being patient with me and my spiritual journey. I know that there must be times where You get frustrated with my faults and my moments of "fooling*

around." Lord, give me the desire and "want-to" to follow You – really follow You. Help me to deny my wants and wishes. Give me the strength to take up my cross Daily and carry it for You! I love You, Praise You, and Adore You. Amen.

I would not be true to my calling, if I did not conclude this book with an opportunity for salvation.

If while reading this book, you have realized that you cannot rededicate your life, because you have never truly dedicated it to Him; you can give Christ your heart and life today. The Bible states it this way:

1. ADMIT THAT YOU ARE A SINNER
- Ro. 3:23 *"for all have sinned and fall short of the glory of God,"*

2. BELIEVE THAT JESUS IS GOD'S SON
- John 3:16 *"For God so loved the world that he gave his one and only Son, that whoever believes in him shall not perish but have eternal life."*

3. CONFESS YOUR SINS TO HIM
- 1 John 1:9 *"If we confess our sins, he is faithful and just and will forgive us our sins and purify us from all unrighteousness."*

4. DEDICATE YOUR LIFE TO HIM

- Ro. 10:9-10 *"That if you confess with your mouth, "Jesus is Lord," and believe in your heart that God raised him from the dead, you will be saved. For it is with your heart that you believe and are justified, and it is with your mouth that you confess and are saved."*

If you would like to make the most important decision of your life; If you are willing to place your faith in God and surrender your life to Him today; you can say a prayer similar to the following:

> *God, I know that I am a sinner, I have messed up in my thoughts and in my actions. But I do believe with all my heart that you died on the cross for my sins and that you rose again to conquer death. Right now, I confess to you that I am sinful. I make a commitment to turn from my sins and turn to You. Please come into my heart and save me! Thank you so much for being patient with me up to this point of my salvation. Please help me to grow up to become all that you would have me be. In the Name of Jesus Christ, your Son, I pray. Amen!*

If you said a prayer like this and you truly meant it

in your heart. Then don't fool around. Tell a friend. Tell twenty! Also, make your decision public through your local church or find a family of faith that you can grow in the Lord with! God Bless you!! Remember, life is too short to fool around! So Follow Him!!

NOTES

Introduction: "Oxymorons for Spiritual Morons"
1. http://www.houstonprofootball.com/team/rb.html
2. Paul Lee Tan, *Encyclopedia of 7,700 Illustrations* (Rockville, Md.: Assurance Publishers, 1979), 1361.
3. Ibid., 581.
4. Jean L. McKechnie, eds., *Webster's New Twentieth Century Dictionary of The English Language Unabridged Second Edition* (USA: World Publishing Co., 1978), 1280.

Chapter 2: "Gracefully Unforgiving"
1. Julia H. Johnston, "Grace Greater Than Our Sins."

Chapter 3: "Faithfully Unfaithful"

1. Gary Bauer and James Dobson, *Children at Risk* (Nashville, TN: Word, 1990), 187-8.
2. http://www.christianglobe.com/Illustrations/ theDetails.asp?whichOne=f&whichFile=faithfulness
3. Ibid.

Chapter 4: "Genuinely Hypocritical"

1. Jean L. McKechnie, eds., *Webster's New Twentieth Century Dictionary of The English Language Unabridged Second Edition* (USA: World Publishing Co., 1978), 896.
2. Raymond McHenry, Publisher *The Best of In Other Words* (Houston, TX: Raymond McHenry, 1996), 310.
3. Jean L. McKechnie, eds., *Webster's New Twentieth Century Dictionary of The English Language Unabridged Second Edition* (USA: World Publishing Co., 1978), 896.
4. *The Best of In Other Words*, Publisher Raymond McHenry. (Houston, TX: Raymond McHenry, 1996), 136.
5. Ibid.
6. Ibid.
7. Ibid., 54-5.
8. Ibid., 205.

Chapter 5: "Happily Unjoyful"

1. http://www.christianglobe.com/Illustrations/
   theDetails.asp?whichOne=f&whichFile=joy
2. Jean L. McKechnie, eds., *Webster's New Twentieth Century Dictionary of The English Language Unabridged Second Edition* (USA: World Publishing Co., 1978), 188.
3. http://www.christianglobe.com/Illustrations/
   theDetails.asp?whichOne=f&whichFile=bitter-ness
4. Jean L. McKechnie, eds., *Webster's New Twentieth Century Dictionary of The English Language Unabridged Second Edition* (USA: World Publishing Co., 1978), 371.
5. http://www.christianglobe.com/Illustrations/
   theDetails.asp?whichOne=f&whichFile=bitter-ness
6. http://www.christianglobe.com/Illustrations/
   theDetails.asp?whichOne=f&whichFile=compla ining
7. http://www.christianglobe.com/Illustrations/
   theDetails.asp?whichOne=f&whichFile=joy

"Another Pause For Perspective"

1. http://www.christianglobe.com/Illustrations/
   theDetails.asp?whichOne=f&whichFile=follower

"Chapter 6: "Evangelistically Un-evangelistic"
1. http://www.christianglobe.com/Illustrations/theDetails.asp?whichOne=f&whichFile=evangelism
2. Ibid.
3. Ibid.
4. Ibid.
5. Ibid.
6. David Larsen, *The Evangelism Mandate* (Wheaton, IL: Crossway Books, 1992), 21.
7. http://www.christianglobe.com/Illustrations/theDetails.asp?whichOne=f&whichFile=evangelism

"Chapter 7: "Competitively Noncompetitive"
1. http://www.christianglobe.com/Illustrations/theDetails.asp?whichOne=f&whichFile=defeat
2. *Paul Harvey's For What It's Worth*, ed. Paul Harvey, Jr. (New York, N.Y.: Bantam Books, 1991), 61.
3. Jean L. McKechnie, eds., *Webster's New Twentieth Century Dictionary of The English Language Unabridged Second Edition* (USA: World Publishing Co., 1978), 370.
4. http://www.christianglobe.com/Illustrations/theDetails.asp?whichOne=f&whichFile=unity
5. http://www.christianglobe.com/Illustrations/theDetails.asp?whichOne=f&whichFile=encouragement
6. http://buffaloblitz.com/blitz_048.htm

"A Preaching For Priority and Perspective"
1. *Greek (UBS) text and Hebrew (BHS) text. PC Study Bible.* Version 3.1 CD-Rom. (Seattle: Biblesoft, 1993-1998)
2. http://private-ryan.eb.com/

Chapter 8: "Arrogantly Humble"
1. http://www.christianglobe.com/Illustrations/theDetails.asp?whichOne=f&whichFile=humility
2. Ibid.
3. Ibid.
4. Ibid.
5. Ibid.
6. Ibid.
7. Ibid.
8. Ibid.
9. Ibid.
10. Ibid.
11. Paul Lee Tan, *Encyclopedia of 7,700 Illustrations* (Rockville, Md.: Assurance Publishers, 1979), 2315.
11. Ibid.
12. http://www.christianglobe.com/Illustrations/theDetails.asp?whichOne=f&whichFile=humility
13. Ibid.
14. Ibid.
15. Ibid.

Chapter 9 "Servant Masters"
1. *Greek (UBS) text and Hebrew (BHS) text. PC Study Bible.* Version 3.1 CD-Rom. (Seattle: Biblesoft, 1993-1998)
2. http://www.christianglobe.com/Illustrations/theDetails.asp?whichOne=f&whichFile=servant
3. Ibid.
4. Ibid.

Chapter 10 "How to Follow Jesus and Stop Fooling Around!"
1. Paul Lee Tan, *Encyclopedia of 7,700 Illustrations* (Rockville, Md.: Assurance Publishers, 1979), 583.
2. Ibid.
3. http://www.abideinchrist.com/messages/jas1v5.html
4. Paul Lee Tan, *Encyclopedia of 7,700 Illustrations* (Rockville, Md.: Assurance Publishers, 1979), 1177.
5. http://www.christianglobe.com/Illustrations/theDetails.asp?whichOne=f&whichFile=sacrifice
6. http://www.christianglobe.com/Illustrations/theDetails.asp?whichOne=f&whichFile=cross
7. Paul Lee Tan, *Encyclopedia of 7,700 Illustrations* (Rockville, Md.: Assurance Publishers, 1979), 297.
8. Ibid., 1177.

9. http://www.famci.com/hearthstone/1998 hearthstones/hstone0698.htm

10. Paul Lee Tan, *Encyclopedia of 7,700 Illustrations* (Rockville, Md.: Assurance Publishers, 1979), 539.

11. Ibid., 1006.

Printed in the United States
928200002B